REVISE FOR CAMBRIDGE UNIVERSITY CERTIFICATES OF ENGLISH

A 500-HUNDERED KEY WORK TRANSFORMATION REVISION

(FOR FIRST B2, ADVANCED C1 & PROFICIENCY C2)

Editora Appris Ltda.
1.ª Edição - Copyright© 2024 do autor
Direitos de Edição Reservados à Editora Appris Ltda.

Nenhuma parte desta obra poderá ser utilizada indevidamente, sem estar de acordo com a Lei nº 9.610/98. Se incorreções forem encontradas, serão de exclusiva responsabilidade de seus organizadores. Foi realizado o Depósito Legal na Fundação Biblioteca Nacional, de acordo com as Leis nos 10.994, de 14/12/2004, e 12.192, de 14/01/2010.

Catalogação na Fonte
Elaborado por: Josefina A. S. Guedes
Bibliotecária CRB 9/870

M183r
2024
	Madureira, Ricardo
	    Revise for Cambridge University certificates of english: a 500-hundered key work transformation revision (for First B2, Advanced C1 & Proficiency C2) / Ricardo Madureira. – 1. ed. – Curitiba: Appris, 2024.
	    186 p. ; 23 cm.
	
	    Inclui referências.
	    ISBN 978-65-250-5823-8
	
	    1. Língua inglesa – Estudo e ensino. 2. Certificados. 3. Universidade de Cambridge. I. Título. II. Série.
	
	                                                    CDD – 428.24

Editora e Livraria Appris Ltda.
Av. Manoel Ribas, 2265 – Mercês
Curitiba/PR – CEP: 80810-002
Tel. (41) 3156 - 4731
www.editoraappris.com.br

Printed in Brazil
Impresso no Brasil

RICARDO MADUREIRA

REVISE FOR CAMBRIDGE UNIVERSITY CERTIFICATES OF ENGLISH

A 500-HUNDERED KEY WORK TRANSFORMATION REVISION

(FOR FIRST B2, ADVANCED C1 & PROFICIENCY C2)

FICHA TÉCNICA

EDITORIAL	Augusto Coelho
	Sara C. de Andrade Coelho
	Marli Caetano
COMITÊ EDITORIAL	Ana El Achkar (UNIVERSO/RJ)
	Andréa Barbosa Gouveia (UFPR)
	Conrado Moreira Mendes (PUC-MG)
	Eliete Correia dos Santos (UEPB)
	Fabiano Santos (UERJ/IESP)
	Francinete Fernandes de Sousa (UEPB)
	Francisco Carlos Duarte (PUCPR)
	Francisco de Assis (Fiam-Faam, SP, Brasil)
	Jacques de Lima Ferreira (UP)
	Juliana Reichert Assunção Tonelli (UEL)
	Maria Aparecida Barbosa (USP)
	Maria Helena Zamora (PUC-Rio)
	Maria Margarida de Andrade (Umack)
	Marilda Aparecida Behrens (PUCPR)
	Roque Ismael da Costa Güllich (UFFS)
	Toni Reis (UFPR)
	Valdomiro de Oliveira (UFPR)
	Valério Brusamolin (IFPR)
SUPERVISOR DA PRODUÇÃO	Renata Cristina Lopes Miccelli
PRODUÇÃO EDITORIAL	William Rodrigues e Adrielli de Almeida
REVISÃO TÉCNICA	Bruna Fernanda Martins
DIAGRAMAÇÃO	Bruno Ferreira Nascimento
CAPA	Julie Lopes

PRESENTATION

OVERVIEW

The **Key Word Transformation** sentences (from now on, KWTs) from the paper **Use of English** can be quite challenging, as the reader is probably already familiar with. I have written this book as a tool to help candidates brush up on what they have already studied, so that they feel more confident when sitting the official examinations.

Structure

This book contains 500 KWTs, distributed as follows:

- Sentences 1 to 150: **First Certificate in English** (B2, upper-intermediate)
- Sentences 151 to 325: **Certificate in Advanced English** (C1) &
- Sentences 326-500: **Certificate of Proficiency in English** (C2) (post-advanced)

Even if you are currently at one of the advanced levels (C1/C2), we highly recommend that you start by doing the B2 sentences (**First**), as they may serve as a warm-up for the more complex sentences ahead (**Advanced** and **Proficiency**). Furthermore, revising is always advisable if you are serious about obtaining your Cambridge certificate. It is not uncommon for more advanced learners to make mistakes at lower levels.

How to Use the Book

Do the KTWs

We suggest that you study the book in the same order as the sentence items appear, as there is no particular gradation of any kind. At any rate, since some of the questions may be a little difficult (or complex, if you will), we would recommend that you plan in advance how many questions you want to answer in a seating.

We may suggest that you do between 6 (actual number of items in the exams) and 10 sentences at a time, considering that you still need to check your answers and possibly do some search to wrap the whole revising process up. If you do not wish to study to such a plan, at least make sure you stop when your powers of concentration start to weaken, since resting also plays an important part in the learning process.

Check Your Answers

After that, check your answers in the **Answer Key** at the end of the book, evaluate your progress, making adaptations to your study plan (if at all necessary) as you move on.

Follow-up

You might want to take a look at the explanatory **notes** that follow some of the answers. These are comments on **grammar**, **spelling**, **(near-) synonyms** and **(near-) antonyms**, **collocation patterns**, **word formation** and/or other general relevant aspects of the English language. Again, even if your answer is correct, as an ambitious candidate/learner, you may well benefit from reading such notes, even if at a brief, quick glance.

ACKNOWLEDGMENTS

I have drawn on the expertise of many experienced coursebook authors, whose work has inspired me to create my own KWTs. Credit has been given to such authors in the **bibliography** at the end of the book. If there remains any failure on our part to do so, do not hesitate to point that out to us. We will be glad to include it in a possible future printed new edition or e-book version.

Piloting

The exercises have been tested at to feasibility by some volunteer "pilots", students attending High School/technical courses at IF Sudeste de Minas Gerais, campus Juiz de Fora, where I work as a teacher of English (and Portuguese). Here they are, in alphabetical order:

David Lessa

He holds the **First Certificate in English** (B2), from Cambridge University (UK), in which he managed to achieve the C1 level (**advanced**) for outstanding performance. D. Lessa contributed by answering some samples from the **FCE** (B2) items. He is a senior, distinguished student who is about to complete High School.

Update: D. Lessa is now enrolled on the course "Control and Automation Engineering" at UFMG (Universidade Federal de Minas Gerais).

Mariana Itaborahy

Mariana is a candidate for **First** (B2) herself and my assistant to the subject of English. She helps me with students with remedial needs. She got this post by being selected in a rigorous process by means of an examination based on Cambridge tests. She also contributed by answering some of the **FCE** sentences.

Max Jabour

Max A. Giancoli Jabour attended a private English course. After finishing it, he was certified by Cambridge University with the **LinguaSkill Certificate**, described as C1 (**advanced** or above). He contributed to this project by answering some samples from **FCE** and **Advanced** (C1). Max is a self-motivated student/learner who aims really high.

Proofreading

Last but not least, I have also counted on the outstanding contribution of my colleague and friend, English teacher José Ricardo Tarôco, as proofreader, who read the whole original and made suggestions, such as improving a sentence or providing another possible answer to an item, among other priceless contributions.

José Ricardo Tarôco

J. R. Tarôco has a degree in "Letras", from Universidade de Uberaba (MG) and is post-graduated (latu sensu) in Linguistics from Unyleia. He holds all the certificates from the Cambridge main suite (from beginning to **CPE**, post-advanced, C2), as well as the TKT (**Teaching Knowledge Certificate**), also from Cambridge University. He is experienced in teaching English to students of all ages, including candidates for Cambridge exams.

Note on the Answers

As far as possible, every effort has been made to ensure that there is only one answer to each item. However, when more than one answer is possible, this has been shown. If you come up with an answer that is completely different from the one(s) given, but you are not sure that it is correct, we would encourage you to write to the publishing house, which will refer your inquiry to the author, who will be glad to help sort it out. If the reader's contribution is also an acceptable answer, we may consider including it in a future edition (whether in print or e-book), giving credit to the contributors.

Dedication Notes

*To my mother (***in memoriam***), my first teacher, beyond school subjects, for always being there for me and for always believing in me.*

To the contributors who took part in the piloting process and proofreading, for their availability, enthusiasm and kindness.

To you, the reader/candidate, who has decided to purchase this book hoping to obtain your Cambridge certificate. I wish you the best of luck!

I hope you enjoy studying this book as much as I have enjoyed writing it.

Best wishes,

Ricardo Madureira

PORT OF ENTRY

You may look forward to reaching your final destination, believing there is where, at long last, you will find happiness, or whatever else you are looking for, but you may well find out that there could be a lot of joy and pleasures along the way, if you would only keep your eyes (and spirit) wide open!

ÍTACA

Konstantinos Kaváfis

Greek Poet (1863-1933)

Quando partires em tua jornada a Ítaca
faz votos de que seja longo o caminho,
cheio de aventuras e de descobertas.
Os Lestrigões e os Ciclopes,
o irascível Poseidon, não os temas,
pois não os encontrarás no caminho,
se elevado é teu pensamento, se única é
a emoção que aflora em teu espírito.
Os Lestrigões e os Ciclopes,
o irascível Poseidon, não os encontrarás,
se já os não levas, desde a partida, em tua alma,
se tua alma já os não traz dentro de ti.

Faz votos de que seja longo o caminho.
Que sejam muitas as manhãs de verão,
quando, com que prazer, com que júbilo,
chegarás a portos nunca d'antes vistos;
Vai aos mercados fenícios

e compra maravilhosas mercadorias,
nácares e corais, âmbares e ébanos
e toda a espécie de perfumes inebriantes,
compra deles tanto quanto possível;
Vai a muitas cidades egípcias,
e aprende, sem cessar, com seus sábios.

Guarda Ítaca em teu pensamento, sempre,
Pois é teu destino ali aportar.
Mas não tenhas pressa em tua jornada.
Que a viagem dure muitos e muitos anos
e que, quando já velho, ancores na ilha,
rico com tudo que ganhaste no caminho,
não esperes que Ítaca te receba com riquezas.

Ítaca deu-te a bela viagem.
Sem ela, jamais te porias a caminho.
Nada mais tem ela a oferecer-te.
Acaso a encontres pobre, Ítaca não te enganou:
Sábio como te tornaste, com tanta bagagem,
Hás de ter compreendido então o que significam Ítacas.

(Nossa tradução livre, para o português,
da versão em inglês, cuja autoria é de Daniel Mendelsohn)

TABLE OF CONTENTS

KWT 1 TO 150
FIRST (B2) 17

KWT 151 TO 325
ADVANCED (C1) 35

KWT 326 TO 500
PROFICIENCY (C2) 61

ANSWER KEY
FIRST (B2) 85
ADVANCED (C1) 103
C2 – PROFICIENCY 126

LANGUAGE BOOSTER 1
Advanced Vocabulary for Michigan Proficiency (C2), IELTS and TOEFL 150

LANGUAGE BOOSTER 2
COMMON PHRASAL VERBS AT B2, C1 & C2 154

LANGUAGE BOOSTER 3
   IDIOMS (BY THEMES) 157

LANGUAGE BOOSTER 4
   BINOMIALS 160

LANGUAGE BOOSTER 5
   DEPEDENT PREPOSITIONS (NOUNS, ADJECTIVES & VERBS) .. 164

LANGUAGE BOOSTER 6
   VERBS WITH DEPENDENT PREPOSITIONS 166

LANGUAGE BOOSTER 7

   DO OR MAKE?... 168

LANGUAGE BOOSTER 8

RARE WORDS... 170

LANGUAGE BOOSTER 9

   SIMILAR EXPRESSIONS IN ENGLISH AND PORTUGUESE.... 171

LANGUAGE BOOSTER 10

   FALSE (AND TRUE) FRIENDS 173

WORD LIST 180

BIBLIOGRAPHY.. 184

KWT 1 to 150

FIRST (B2)

Complete the second sentence so that it has a similar meaning to the first sentence, as in the example.

➡ You <u>must</u> use between **2** and **5** words.
➡ Do <u>not</u> change the key word in any way. (given in brackets, capital letters, bold type).
➡ Short forms (*isn't, don't, didn't, won't, couldn't...* etc.) count as two words (you may use either one). The genitive (Peter's, children's, today's... etc.) counts as one word only.

Example:

I don't know the answer, so I can't help you. (**WOULD**)
If I _____ help you.
Answer key ↪ If I **_knew the answer, I would_** help you.

1. The plane took off before I got to the airport. (**ALREADY**)
When I got to the airport, the plane _____ off.

2. I didn't understand what he said because he spoke very fast. (**TOO**)
He spoke _____ understand what he said.

3. He will never come here again. (**LAST**)
This is the _____ here.

4. Do you think you can convince him to take part in the scheme? (**INTO**)
Do you think you can talk _____ part in the scheme?

5. I persuaded her not to take part in the fraudulent scheme. (**OUT**)
I _____ part in the fraudulent scheme.

6. I bought this car two years ago. (HAD)
I _____ two years.

7. I'm dying to go on a tour of Brazil. (FORWARD)
I am _____ on a tour of Brazil.

8. When she was younger, Ann didn't like to read. (USE)
Ann _____ when she was younger.

9. I've had English classes since the beginning of the year. (STUDYING)
I _____ English since the beginning of the year.

10. I've never tried snails before. (HAVE)
This is the first time I _____snails.

11. Danny spoke to Paula, and then she found out he had had an accident. (UNTIL)
Paula didn't find out Danny had _____ spoke to her.

12. She really regrets not having enrolled for the examination. (WISHES)
She _____for the examination.

13. John decided to go to bed because he was utterly exhausted. (THAT)
John was _____ he decided to go to bed.

14. I kept trying, but I knew it was no use. (EVEN)
I kept trying, _____ I knew it was no use.

15. 'Well done for passing your finals, Susan', said her teacher. (CONGRATULATED)
Susan _____ finals by her teacher.

16. 'I didn't help you because you lied to me,' he said. (HELPED)
'I _____ you hadn't lied to me,' he said.

17. If you had told me, I might have been able to help you. (**ONLY**)
If _____ told me, I might have been able to help you.

18. This is the first time Richard has visited Brazil. (**VISIT**)
This is Richard's _____ to Brazil.

19. Sandra and Paul were arguing fiercely when I arrived. (**ARGUMENT**)
Sandra was _____ Paul when I arrived.

20. Those children's parents live near me. (**WHOSE**)
Those are _____ live near me.

21. Given the circumstances, the only thing we could do was help. (**BUT**)
We had _____ help.

22. My motorbike is in very bad condition, so it won't last much longer. (**SUCH**)
My motorbike is _____ it won't last much longer.

23. It was careless of us to leave without closing the windows. (**SHOULD**)
We _____ the windows before we left.

24. If the sun is shining, we're going to the beach at the weekend. (**UNLESS**)
We're going to the beach at the weekend, _____ shining.

25. We're going to the beach, unless it is raining. (**NOT**)
We're going to the beach if _____ raining.

26. Do you have any plans for the weekend? (**GOING**)
What _____ at the weekend?

27. We will get to the cinema after the beginning of the film. (**HAVE**)
By the time we get to the cinema, _____ begun.

28. 'Does this bus go to the university?' (**GOES**)
Could you tell me _____ to the university?

29. He said, 'I'll give you a lift to work.' (**ME**)
He said he _____ a lift to work.

30. 'That's false! I've never been expelled from school,' said Tina. (**HAVING**)
Tina denied _____ from school.

31. We haven't been to the cinema for ages. (**SINCE**)
It's ages _____ to the cinema.

32. The last time I was in Paris was in 2015. (**BEEN**)
I _____ Paris since 2015.

33. This is my first experience as an air traveller. (**NEVER**)
I _____ by plane before.

34. When did they start to go out together? (**GOING**)
How _____ out together?

35. I will have to manage without taking a holiday abroad this year. (**DO**)
I will have to _____ a holiday abroad this year.

36. I haven't found time to answer your e-mail yet. (**ROUND**)
I still haven't _____ your e-mail yet.

37. The hotel's service was atrocious, but the meals were sumptuous. (**MADE**)
The hotel's sumptuous meals _____ its atrocious service.

38. 'I'm afraid I'm a bit indisposed to go out, Sally,' answered Joe. (**UP**)
Joe told sally he was _____out.

39. After working hard, I was eager to have a substantial meal. (**MOOD**)
After working hard, I was _____
a substantial meal.

40. You should've already learned to defend yourself by now. (**STAND**)
It's high time you _____ yourself.

41. On my way back home from work, I paid a friend a short visit. (**CALLED**)
I _____ a friend on my way back home from work.

42. I almost never get the recognition I think I deserve. (**DO**)
Seldom _____ the recognition I think I deserve.

43. I realised only then that I had lost my wallet. (**REALISE**)
Only then _____ that I had lost my wallet.

44. Never forget to close the windows under any circumstances. (**SHOULD**)
Under _____ to close the windows.

45. 'I will not tolerate your unacceptable behaviour any longer,' my father said to me. (**PUT**)
My father said to me that he would _____
my unacceptable behaviour.

46. We don't have much time left, so we'd better work faster. (**RUNNING**)
We'd better work faster because we're _____ time.

47. The student didn't once offer his teacher a word of apology. (**OFFER**)
Not _____ his teacher a word of apology.

48. Putting myself in your situation, I'd look for medical help. (**WERE**)
If _____, I'd look for medical help.

49. Under no circumstances should this door be opened during the flight. (**NOT**)
This door should _____ circumstances during the flight.

50. Have you thought of a solution to the problem yet? (**COME**)
Have you _____ a solution to the problem yet?

51. If the weather isn't favourable, we'll cancel the match. (**OFF**)
If the weather isn't favourable, we'll _____ the match.

52. I'll give you a guided tour of the city, what do you think? (**AROUND**)
Shall _____ the city?

53. How about postponing the meeting until next week? (**PUTTING**)
How about _____ until next week?

54. 'Keep our secret to yourself, will you?' Susan asked her friend. (**GIVE**)
Susan asked her friend _____ away.

55. I think Joe has eaten less chocolate because he's much fitter now. (**CUT**)
Joe _____ chocolate because he's much fitter now.

56. My teacher suggested I should study languages to enhance my memory. (**ADVISED**)
I _____ languages to enhance my memory by my teacher.

57. The novel was so exciting that I just couldn't put it down. (**SUCH**)
It _____ that I just couldn't put it down.

58. Students quite often arrive late. **(COMMON)**
It _____ to arrive early.

59. Henry doesn't find it strange to work in groups any more. **(USED)**
Henry has _____ in groups now.

60. I'm looking forward to going on holiday. **(DYING)**
I _____ on holiday.

61. Studying hard is a new experience for her. **(USED)**
She has _____ hard yet.

62. Did she study hard when she was at university? **(USE)**
Did _____ hard when she was at university?

63. Jane always found it difficult to give her students a scold. **(USED)**
Jane just couldn't _____ her students a scold.

64. I badly need a holiday. I'm completely worn out. **(DO)**
I could _____ a holiday. I'm completely worn out.

65. They had their house redecorated, and then moved in. **(UP)**
They _____, and then moved in.

66. The government has promised to abolish capital punishment. **(AWAY)**
The government has promised to _____ capital punishment.

67. I don't usually go out at weekends. **(UNUSUAL)**
It is _____ out at weekends.

68. When I was a kid, I usually walked to school. **(WOULD)**
When I was a kid, I _____ to school.

69. Before then, the children had never had to put their toys away. (**EVER**)
That was the first time the children _____
to put their toys away.

70. How long will it be before you've finished your homework? (**TAKE**)
How long _____ to finish
your homework?

71. I'm finding it difficult to get all my work done punctually. (**DIFFICULTY**)
I _____ all my work done
punctually.

72. I have never read a better book than this one. (**FAR**)
This _____ I have read.

73. 'The manager will investigate your complaints as soon as possible,' the receptionist told me. (**LOOKED**)
I was told by the receptionist that my complaints _____
_____ the manager as soon as possible.

74. Last year, unfavourable weather conditions caused the postponement of the championship. (**BECAUSE**)
Last year, the championship _____
unfavourable weather conditions.

75. Jonh does not want to continue to work for this company any more. (**CARRY**)
John no _____ working for
this company.

76. The rate of crime has not increased so far this year. (**INCREASE**)
There _____ the rate of
crime so far this year.

77. I cannot get all my suitcases into the baggage compartment. (**BIG**)
The baggage compartment is _____ take all my suitcases.

78. I couldn't get to school on time because of the slow traffic. (**PREVENTED**)
The slow traffic _____ to school on time.

79. He tiptoed into the house very quietly so that he wouldn't wake up anyone. (**AVOID**)
He tiptoed into the house very quietly so _____
_____ up.

80. Sam studied really hard so that she would get a good grade. (**ORDER**)
Sam studied really hard _____ a good grade.

81. I think this rain has come to stay for the weekend. (**SET**)
I think this rain has _____ for the weekend.

82. You have to fill in this form by Friday at the latest. (**FILLED**)
This form _____ by Friday at the latest.

83. He trained very hard in order to be fit for the competition. (**WOULD**)
He trained very hard so _____ fit for the competition.

84. You shouldn't eat chocolate if you're on a diet. (**OUGHT**)
You _____ chocolate if you're on a diet.

85. Candidates shouldn't leave the examination room without permission. (**ALLOWED**)
Candidates _____ the examination room without permission.

86. I think she should start doing physical exercise immediately. (**HAD**)
I think she _____ physical exercise immediately.

87. 'You must leave immediately, Sarah!' said the teacher. (**HAD**)
The teacher told Sarah _____ immediately.

88. Stop interrupting me, will you? It's so annoying! (**WISH**)
I _____ interrupting me.

89. It wasn't necessary for us to resit the test, but we did. (**NEEDN'T**)
We _____ the test, but we did.

90. Mike is late. Perhaps he missed the bus. (**MIGHT**)
Mike is late. He _____ the bus.

91. I was supposed to leave earlier, but that wasn't possible. (**LEFT**)
I was to _____ earlier, but that wasn't possible.

92. I'm sure it wasn't him that you saw. He's gone to Rome on holiday. (**CAN'T**)
It _____ you saw. He's gone to Rome on holiday.

93. I'm almost sure I've left my keys back at the office. (**MUST**)
I _____ my keys back at the office.

94. Candidates are welcome to contact us if they need more information. (**TOUCH**)
'Candidates, feel comfortable to _____ us if you need more information,' she told us.

95. I didn't buy the book because it was too expensive. (**BOUGHT**)
I _____ the book if it hadn't been so expensive.

96. During the examination, I just couldn't think of the correct answer to the question. (**COME**)
During the examination, I was not _____ the correct answer to the question.

97. We continued to walk despite heavy snow starting to fall. (**EVEN**)
We kept on _____ started to snow heavily.

98. Almost all the tickets for the play on Broadway have been sold. (**HARDLY**)
There are _____ for the play on Broadway.

99. Do you think it is likely that Rob will pass the exams he has signed up for? (**CHANCE**)
Do you think Rob _____ the exams he has signed up for?

100. 'Do you know the cost of the tickets?' Henry asked me. (**MUCH**)
Henry asked me If I _____ were.

101. We had to complete all the tasks before we could leave. (**COMPLETED**)
We couldn't _____ all the tasks.

102. We had not expected the conversations to be so animated. (**BETTER**)
The conversations _____ expected.

103. If Phil doesn't train harder, he'll never make the team. (**DOES**)
Phil will never make the team unless _____ more training.

104. She asked me, 'What do you think of the party?' (**LIKE**)
She asked me, 'How _____ the party?'

27

105. I signed up for the proficiency examination a month ago. **(SINCE)**
It _____ I signed up for the examination.

106. They say the notorious criminals fled to Mexico. **(HAVE)**
The notorious criminals _____ to Mexico.

107. Because of the demonstrations, the police wouldn't let us park in the city centre. **(ALLOWED)**
We _____ in the city centre because of the demonstrations.

108. 'Did you see the new film released last weekend?' my boyfriend asked me. **(SEEN)**
My boyfriend wanted to _____ the new film released last weekend.

109. Whatever you say, I won't believe you. **(MATTER)**
I won't believe you, no _____ say.

110. Maybe the students have forgotten that the time of the meeting was changed. **(MIGHT)**
The students _____ that the time of the meeting was changed.

111. My mother made me stay up late to cram for an examination. **(TO)**
I _____ up late by my mother to cram for an examination.

112. My grandparents were determined to pay for our holidays. **(INSISTED)**
My grandparents _____ for our holidays.

113. I failed to persuade my students to sign up for the exams. **(SUCCEED)**
I _____ my students to sign up for the exams.

114. 'I would prefer you not to use your phone on the train,' the mother told her daughter. (**MIND**)
The mother told her daughter, 'Would _____ your phone on the train?'

115. 'Don't leave yet, will you?' she asked me. (**RATHER**)
I would _____ yet.

116. This student sometimes finds it difficult to stick to rules. (**TROUBLE**)
This student sometimes _____ to rules.

117. 'Do you think Angela is likely to change her mind?' Jane asked. (**CHANCE**)
Jane asked, 'Is there _____ her mind?'

118. You ought to have filled up the tank before we left. (**CARELESS**)
It was _____ have filled up the tank before we left.

119. Paula is the only student who has replied to the e-mail so far. (**NOBODY**)
Apart _____ has replied to the e-mail so far.

120. More people live in urban areas nowadays than in the countryside. (**MANY**)
Nowadays, there are _____ in the countryside as in urban areas.

121. I have a suspicion that he is not a dependable colleague. (**SUSPECT**)
I _____ a dependable colleague.

122. That's the hotel where we stayed last year. (**IN**)
That's the hotel _____ last year.

123. I don't like Pete because he's very mean. (**REASON**)
Pete's _____ why I don't like him.

124. I intended to leave earlier, but I decided to finish some reports instead. (**GOING**)
I _____ earlier, but I decided to finish some reports instead.

125. The father of that boy is a highly celebrated actor. (**WHOSE**)
That's _____ a highly celebrated actor.

126. I didn't have much money, but we were happy because we had each other. (**HAVING**)
In spite _____ much money, we were happy because we had each other.

127. We enjoyed the camping trip, even though the weather was awful. (**SPITE**)
We enjoyed the camping trip, _____ that the weather was awful.

128. I don't like camping very much. I'd rather stay in a comfortable hotel. (**KEEN**)
I am _____ camping. I'd rather stay in a comfortable hotel.

129. M. de Assis was an extremely talented Brazilian writer. (**BRAZIL'S**)
M. de Assis was one of _____ writers.

130. The Empire State building is not as tall as The World Trade Center. (**THAN**)
The World Trade Center building _____ the Empire State.

131. It's a lot easier to learn a language by picking it up on the streets than from books alone. (**MUCH**)
You can learn a language _____
when you pick it up on the streets than from books alone.

132. There's no point in arguing any further. (**POINTLESS**)
It _____ any further.

133. It's impossible to put into words what I felt. (**NOT**)
What _____ to put into words.

134. If I accept this job, I'll have to commute into the city centre every day. (**MEAN**)
Accepting this job _____ into the city centre every day.

135. Sarah is regretful that she gave up school so easily. (**HAVING**)
Sarah _____ school so easily.

136. Eric admitted that he had stolen the money. (**TO**)
Eric admitted _____ stolen the money.

137. 'How about going to the cinema?' she asked us. (**SHALL**)
She said, 'Let's _____ we?'

138. I've found some old pictures by chance in a drawer. (**ACROSS**)
I have _____ some old pictures in a drawer.

139. 'I'll drive if you feel like a rest, Dad,' his daughter said. (**OVER**)
The daughter offered to take _____ like a rest.

140. They didn't once offer us a word of support. (**WERE**)
Not once _____ a word of support.

141. Whatever is the time? (**EARTH**)
What _____ the time?

142. Both of the vending machines were out of order. (**OF**)
Neither _____ working.

143. Your nails need trimming. (**GET**)
You _____ trimmed.

144. You will avoid many problems if you make your reservation in advance. (**ADVISABLE**)
It would _____ made your reservation in advance.

145. I have never come across such a terrible book before. (**WORST**)
This is _____ ever come across.

146. By next year, Jones will be celebrating thirty years in the field of English teaching. (**WORKING**)
By next year, Jones _____ in the field of English teaching for thirty years.

147. The idea of dying can be frightening for many people. (**FRIGHTENED**)
A lot of people _____ the idea of dying.

148. No fewer than five assistants are needed to help. (**LEAST**)
We _____ assistants to help.

149. 'Can I borrow your book?' he asked. (**LEND**)
He asked me _____ my book.

150. I cannot stop myself from crying when I read this author's novels. (**HELP**)
I cannot _____ cry when I read this author's novels.

END OF KWT B2. GO ON TO C1. ➡ ➡ ➡ ➡ ➡ ➡ ➡ ➡ ➡

KWT 151 to 325

ADVANCED (C1)

Complete the second sentence so that it has a similar meaning to the first sentence, as in the example.

- You <u>must</u> use between **3** and **6** words.
- Do <u>not</u> change the key word in any way. (given in brackets, capital letters, bold type).
- Short forms (*isn't, don't, didn't, won't, couldn't...* etc.) count as two words (you may use either one) The genitive (*Peter's, children's, today's...* etc.) counts as one word only.

Example:

I didn't know the answer, so I couldn't help her. (**HAVE**)
If I had _____ help her.
Answer key ↪ If I had **_known the answer I would have_** been able to help her.

151. It is highly unlikely that I will pass the driving test. (**ODDS**)
The _____ the driving test.

152. Call on us any time you're around. (**HAPPEN**)
If you _____ around, call on us.

153. If he worked harder, would you recommend him for promotion? (**WORK**)
Were _____ harder, would you recommend him for promotion?

154. I had just reached the car when it began to pour with rain. (**THAN**)
No sooner _____ it began to pour with rain.

35

155. I wanted to get a painter to redo my bedroom before I travelled, but I didn't have the time. (**HAD**)
I would like _____ before I travelled, but I didn't have the time.

156. 'John wrote the song, not George,' Paul said. (**IT**)
According to Paul, _____ the song, not George.

157. I knew nothing at all about who the package belonged to. (**ABSOLUTELY**)
I had _____ it was.

158. Even if it is expensive, they want to stay at the five-star hotel. (**MAY**)
Expensive _____, they want to stay at the five-star hotel.

159. Unless someone is late, we should be able to cover all the points in today's lesson. (**TURNS**)
So long _____ time, we should be able to cover all the points in today's lesson.

160. If you don't tell truth, the camping trip will be cancelled. (**MEAN**)
Your failure to tell _____ the camping trip.

161. My sister works much harder than I do. (**NOWHERE**)
I'm _____ my sister is.

162. It's the first time she has been here, so it is possible that she got lost. (**HAVE**)
She _____ it is the first time she has been here.

163. 'How long will it take for Mark to recover from his illness, Peter?' asked Jane. (**GET**)
Jane asked Peter how long he thought it _____ _____ over his illness.

164. Joe regretted speaking so bluntly to his teacher. (**MORE**)
Joe wished _____ tactfully to his teacher.

165. You really have to make a decision about your future. (**MIND**)
It's high _____ about your future.

166. 'Complete your assignments first, and then you can hang out with your friends,' my father said. (**LONG**)
My father agreed to let me hang out with my friends _____ _____ my assignments first.

167. People think the terrorists have fled from the country. (**THOUGHT**)
The terrorists _____ from the country.

168. Henry thought of organizing a house-warming party for the new neighbours. (**CAME**)
Henry _____ organizing a house-warming party for the new neighbours.

169. Thanks to the scholarship, I got into university. (**FOR**)
If it _____ the scholarship, I wouldn't have got into university.

170. They're decorating my room, so it is in an awful mess. (**DONE**)
I am _____, so it is in an awful mess.

171. When his car broke down, Michael phoned a mechanic. (**DID**)
When his car broke down, what _____ a mechanic.

172. It has been reported that there are massive landslides blocking the motorway. (**REPORTS**)
There _____ massive landslides blocking the motorway.

173. It seems that his participation in the scheme is not evident at all. (**APPEARS**)
There _____ whatsoever that he participated in the scheme.

174. It seems that there is no evidence to support the accusations made against him. (**SEEM**)
There _____ evidence to support the accusations made against him.

175. There are a few aspects of my job that I don't like, but by and large I enjoy it. (**WHOLE**)
Though there are a few aspects of my job that I don't like, _____ I enjoy it.

176. It's useless to try to make him change his mind, as he is very stubborn. (**USE**)
There _____ to make him change his mind, as he is very stubborn.

177. My parents allow me to do almost everything, but they don't let me drink or smoke. (**LINE**)
My parents allow me to do almost everything, but they _____ or smoking.

178. I absolutely hate it when my teachers talk down to me, as if I were an idiot. (**BEING**)
I strongly object _____ my teachers, as if I were an idiot.

179. She will just avert her gaze whenever her father tells her off for her unseemly behaviour. (**AWAY**)
She will just _____ her father whenever he tells her off for her unseemly behaviour.

180. If he keeps neglecting his professional duties like that, he'll lose his job. (**FIRED**)
He'll _____ his job if he keeps neglecting his professional duties like that.

181. The children weren't listening to their parents, but they didn't mind. (**ATTENTION**)
The children weren't _____ were saying, but they didn't mind.

182. Given that Ann has no experience, will she be able to carry out such an ambitious project? (**AFFECT**)
Will Ann's _____ to carry out such an ambitious project?

183. 'We won't make any changes to the project for the time being,' my boss said. (**WHATSOEVER**)
My boss said no _____ to the project for the time being.

184. 'Don't forget to keep in touch,' said my friend as he got in the car and drove off. (**NOT**)
My friend reminded _____ in touch as he got in the car and drove off.

185. He no longer thinks he can get a pass grade until the end of the semester. (**HOPE**)
He's given _____ a pass grade until the end of the semester.

186. 'Send my regards to your parents, won't you?' my friend asked me. **(REMEMBER)**
My friend asked me, '_____, won't you?'

187. I don't think the family business will make substantial profits this year, considering the economic situation. **(SURPRISED)**
Considering the economic situation, I _____ _____ the family business made any profits this year.

188. We have no intention of making changes to the academic programme. **(AHEAD)**
The academic programme will _____ _____ to plan.

189. I don't know what I would've done in the same situation as you. **(BEEN)**
Had _____ the same situation as you, I don't know what I would've done.

190. I was just about to leave when the telephone rang. **(POINT)**
I was _____ when the telephone rang.

191. Her boss told her that no one should be allowed to interrupt the meeting. **(CIRCUMSTANCES)**
'Under _____ to be interrupted,' her boss told her.

192. Although the players train really hard, they never make it to the finals. **(MATTER)**
They never make it to the finals, _____ _____ the players train.

193. Despite her best efforts, she never seems to get good grades. **(HOWEVER)**
She never seems to get good grades, _____ tries.

194. The teachers rarely seem to consider the needs of the students. (**ACCOUNT**)
The students' needs rarely _____ by the teachers.

195. Sarah's father said it was her own fault the party was ruined. (**PUT**)
Sarah's father _____ the party being ruined.

196. I'm sorry I said that you looked ugly in your new dress. (**BACK**)
I _____ you looking ugly in your new dress.

197. There were far too many people at the party, but I still had a great time. (**MAY**)
There _____ people at the party, but I still had a great time.

198. 'You've left my mobile phone on the bus, Jane!' Sandra shouted. (**ACCUSED**)
Jane _____ mobile phone on the bus.

199. Although he didn't have any experience, Robert was offered the position. (**SPITE**)
Robert was offered the position, _____ _____ complete inexperience.

200. There were far too many applicants for the position, but we chose only a few to be interviewed. (**SHORTLISTED**)
There were far too many applicants for the position, but only a few _____ interview.

201. I don't usually judge the way people speak, but I couldn't help noticing his pronounced accent. (**HABIT**)
I'm not _____ manner of speaking, but I couldn't help noticing his pronounced accent.

202. There were many wonderful compositions, but only three received special praise. (**SINGLED**)
There were many wonderful compositions, but only three _____ _____ special praise.

203. He should have learned to fend for himself by now. (**HIGH**)
It's _____ to fend for himself.

204. I'm not really sure, but I'd say it'll be very expensive. (**HEAD**)
Off the _____, I'd say it'll be very expensive.

205. He's studying hard in order to obtain a scholarship at college. (**VIEW**)
He's studying hard _____ a scholarship at college.

206. If Richard withdraws from the race, Peter might come out victorious. (**STANDS**)
If Richard withdraws from the race, Peter _____ _____ out victorious.

207. I'm completely sure your parents are already in the know about everything by now. (**BOUND**)
Your parents _____ out about everything by now.

208. If you want this job, you must be able to think and make decisions quickly. (**FEET**)
The _____ is essential if you want this job.

209. It appears that the financial climate will start to look up very soon. (**INDICATION**)
There is _____ that the financial climate will start to look up very soon.

210. I feel better now that I have opened up about my feelings. (**CHEST**)
Now that I _____, I feel better.

211. The event will very likely be called off. (**LIKELIHOOD**)
There _____ being called off.

212. It is certain that people will protest against the demolition of that historic building. (**BOUND**)
There are _____ against the demolition of that historic building.

213. My daughter was almost crying when I broke the bad news to her. (**VERGE**)
My daughter was _____ down in tears when I broke the bad news to her.

214. I only read that book because it was recommended to me. (**IF**)
I would _____ it hadn't been recommended to me.

215. It seems as though we completely misunderstood what the purpose of our mission was. (**HAVE**)
There seems _____ about the purpose of our mission.

216. There are rumours that the corrupt politician involved in the scandals has already submitted his resignation. (**RUMOURED**)
The corrupt politician _____ in his resignation already.

217. If you hadn't helped me, I wouldn't have been able to complete the task. (**OTHERWISE**)
Thank you for your help, _____ the task.

218. If you insist on going to sleep late, naturally you'll feel tired all day. (**GO**)
If _____ late, naturally you'll feel tired all day.

219. A true story provides the basis for the film about that singer. (**BASED**)
The film about that singer _____
 a true story.

220. If Julia hadn't supported and encouraged us, they would've turned down our project.
(**SUPPORT**)
But _____, they would've turned down our project.

221. She always confides in her best friend. (**TRUSTS**)
She always _____ secrets.

222. A recent study found that there's a link between stress and heart disease. (**BORNE**)
The link between stress and heart disease _____
_____ findings of a recent study.

223. I am not strong enough to lift this heavy box. (**STRONGER**)
If I _____ to lift that heavy box.

224. Don't you think you'd benefit from a few days off? (**DO**)
Don't you think a _____ a lot of good?

225. We have given school supplies to the poorer students. (**PROVIDED**)
The poorer students _____ school supplies.

226. Can you explain how the money disappeared? (**ACCOUNT**)
How _____ of the money?

227. Rick is in the seventh grade now because he didn't pass his finals last year. (**WOULD**)
Rick _____ now if he had passed his finals last year.

228. People generally believe the old church dates from the tenth century. (**WIDELY**)
The old church _____ from the tenth century.

229. He succeeded in talking his classmates into taking part in his project. (**MANAGED**)
He _____ his classmates into taking part in his project.

230. She is not as mean as people believe she is. (**MADE**)
She's not as mean as she _____ be.

231. They resolved to bring the issue up at the next meeting. (**WOULD**)
It _____ be brought up at the next meeting.

232. 'I haven't smoked for a long time,' he told me. (**STOPPED**)
He told me that he _____ ago.

233. She's proud of the fact that she's always early for appointments. (**PRIDES**)
She _____ late for appointments.

234. Please hold on a moment, and I'll get back to you right away. (**WILL**)
If _____ a moment, I'll get back to you right away.

235. Who do you think accounts for the failure of the project? (**HELD**)
Who do you think is _____ the project going wrong?

236. 'You can't use the office computers for anything except work', my boss said. (**MEANT**)
My boss said we were _____ the office computers for anything except work.

237. Apart from Michael, no other teachers were selected for the course overseas. (**BE**)
Michael _____ selected for the course overseas.

238. He enjoyed the film, but he wondered whether the events depicted were historically accurate. (**ACCURATELY**)
Although he enjoyed the film, he wasn't sure _____ _____ were.

239. If you hadn't given me a helping hand, I wouldn't have got all the work done. (**GIVING**)
But _____ me a helping hand, I wouldn't have got all the work done.

240. No matter how hard he studied, he never succeeded in getting an honour pass. (**THOUGH**)
Hard _____, he never succeeded in getting an honour pass.

241. The teacher gave me his word that he would allow me to resit the exam. (**ASSURED**)
The teacher _____ allowed to resit the exam.

242. The employee never really thought that he would end up being promoted. (**CROSSED**)
It never _____ mind that he would end up being promoted.

243. The students were impressed by their teacher's ability to remember all of their names. (**ABLE**)
The students found it _____ to remember all of their names.

244. The notorious criminal disappeared with absolutely no indication of his whereabouts. (**TRACE**)
The notorious criminal disappeared, _____ _____ whereabouts.

245. 'I'm sure the other witnesses' testimony will lend support to mine,' the defendant said. (**BEAR**)
The defendant said that the other witnesses' testimony _____ _____ said.

246. Whatever time she leaves home, Lucy never seems to be able to get to school on time. (**MATTER**)
No _____ off from home, Lucy never seems to be able to get to school on time.

247. It is Chris's responsibility to ensure that all the equipment is working properly before the concerts. (**CHARGE**)
Chris's _____ that all the equipment is working properly before the concerts.

248. George was going to throw a house-warming party to welcome the new neighbours, but apparently he's decided against it. (**MIND**)
It appears _____ about throwing a party to welcome the new neighbours.

249. You're re forever changing your mind, John! I can't understand you. (**FIGURE**)
You're forever changing your mind; that's why I can't _____ _____, John.

250. He was looking forward to visiting Paris again. (**HARDLY**)
He _____ Paris again.

47

251. You must have confused me with someone else. (MISTAKEN)
I think _____ someone else.

252. Paul prides himself on always being on time for work. (PRIDE)
Paul takes _____ late for work.

253. What is the exact difference between advanced and proficiency certificates? (DIFFER)
How _____ to proficiency?

254. In the end, it's all a matter of power and status. (DOWN)
In the end, it _____ power and status.

255. How on earth did she deceive you with her story? (TAKEN)
However could _____ her story?

256. They blamed the accident on a cursory inspection of the vehicle. (SAID)
A cursory inspection of the vehicle was _____
_____ the accident.

257. The total came to just over five thousand pounds. (WORKED)
The total _____ just over five thousand pounds.

258. I still haven't fully understood how I succeeded in passing the exam. (SUNK)
It _____ how I managed to pass the exam.

259. We eventually had to take a taxi to the airport. (ENDED)
We _____ a taxi to the airport.

260. He was given the axe because he was involved in an embezzling scheme. (**ACCOUNT**)
He was given the axe _____ involvement in an embezzling scheme.

261. I'll be speaking as a representative of the company which I work for. (**BEHALF**)
I'll be speaking _____ which I work for.

262. He called pretending that he needed to borrow some books, but I knew he was lying. (**PRETENCE**)
He called _____ to borrow some books, but I knew he was lying.

263. Joel was the ideal candidate, so not surprisingly he was awarded the scholarship. (**CAME**)
Joel was the ideal candidate, so it _____ he was awarded the scholarship.

264. There has been a drop in the price of petrol over the last few months. (**COME**)
The price of petrol _____ over the last few months.

265. 'Surely the sun will be scorching hot later, so why don't you apply some sunscreen?' she warned me. (**BETTER**)
She warned me, 'You _____ some sunscreen on. Surely the sun will be scorching hot later.'

266. 'You should stop your students using their mobile phones during the classes,' Mary's colleague told her. (**LET**)
Mary's colleague advised her _____ their mobile phones during the classes.

267. Harry missed his train because we was late leaving for the station. (**LEFT**)
If only _____ time for the station, he wouldn't have missed his train.

268. The guidelines for students' conduct in class need to be thoroughly revised. (**THOROUGH**)
There _____ to the guidelines for students' conduct in class.

269. The unemployment rate dropped gradually as the economy began to improve. (**GRADUAL**)
There _____ the unemployment rate as the economy began to improve.

270. The changes to the exam format didn't make any difference to the candidates. (**CONSEQUENCE**)
The changes to the exam format weren't _____ _____ to the candidates.

271. His colleagues regarded him so highly that he had everyone's support. (**HELD**)
He was _____ by his colleagues that he had everyone's support.

272. We owe our clients some compensation, as we apparently gave them incorrect information. (**APPEAR**)
We owe our clients some compensation, as they _____ _____ given incorrect information.

273. If he passes his entrance exams, which is unlikely, he'll study at one of the Ivy League universities. (**EVENT**)
In the _____ his entrance exams, he'll study at one of the Ivy League universities.

274. Please make sure all our customers are satisfied with the hotel's service. (**SEE**)
Please _____ all our customers are satisfied with the hotel's service.

275. The director insisted that it might be a good idea if he participated in an intensive training programme. (**TAKE**)
The director insisted _____ in an intensive training program.

276. This film has a very strong chance of being nominated for the prize. (**HIGHLY**)
It is _____ be nominated for the prize.

277. 'You really must spend the weekend with us,' she told us. (**SPENDING**)
She insisted _____ the weekend with them.

278. If my sister hadn't told my father about the prang, he wouldn't have argued with me. (**FOR**)
Had it _____ my father about the prang, he wouldn't have argued with me.

279. We were never aware at any moment that we were breaking the law. (**TIME**)
At _____ aware that we were breaking the law.

280. The students are on very good terms with their teachers. (**GET**)
The students _____ with their teachers.

281. They believe Sarah failed her driving test because she was very nervous. (**DOWN**)
Sarah's failure in her driving test _____ nervousness.

282. 'Why didn't I ask him out? He might have accepted!' thought Jane. (**ASKED**)
'If _____ him out, he might have accepted!' thought Jane.

283. Even though he had been severely injured in the accident, he recovered completely. (**PULL**)
He managed _____, even though he had been severely injured in the accident.

284. 'I absolutely hate what the critics are writing about my songs,' Billy said. (**OBJECTED**)
Billy _____ written about his songs by the critics.

285. When he started his course, he soon realised that he had made the wrong choice. (**LONG**)
It did not _____ he had made the wrong choice when he started his course.

286. We could always rely on Joel to confront our teacher if she became too authoritarian. (**STAND**)
Joel could always be _____ our teacher if she became too authoritarian.

287. We can't just pretend that everything will turn out all right in the end. (**DECEIVE**)
We can't just _____ that everything will turn out all right in the end.

288. I don't understand! You can't have watched the same film as I have. (**BEEN**)
I don't understand! It _____ the same film that you watched.

289. I had no interest whatsoever in the offer. (**LEAST**)
I wasn't _____ in the offer.

290. It is not certain that the tournament will take place. (**MEANS**)
It is _____ not the tournament will take place.

291. I tried many times; it was useless to warn him, though. (**TRIED**)
I tried _____ it was useless to warn him.

292. I absolutely hate summer colds. In winter, they seem less nasty. (**STAND**)
What _____ summer colds. In winter, they seem less nasty.

293. Their house was the last house one would expect to be broken into. (**VERY**)
Theirs _____ one would expect to be broken into.

294. One month passed before they published the results. (**UNTIL**)
Not _____ they publish the results.

295. I know you're under a lot of pressure, but don't vent your anger on me. (**OUT**)
I know you're under a lot of pressure, but I wish you _____ me.

296. I apologise in advance, but I have to touch on this thorny issue. (**BRING**)
I apologise in advance, but I _____ this thorny issue.

297. The writer has received a lot of criticism from the more discerning readers. (COME)
The writer _____ a lot of criticism from the more discerning readers.

298. You need to save some money that you can use as a last resort. (FALL)
You need some money to _____ as a last resort.

299. In the end, the students managed to avoid being punished harshly. (LIGHT)
The students got _____ punishment in the end.

300. I'm pressed for time at work to meet tight deadlines. (CLOCK)
I _____ to meet tight deadlines at work.

301. He sometimes found it difficult to make himself understood. (MEANING)
Sometimes he had _____ across.

302. I wish I could give my boss a piece of my mind and then hand in my notice. (MIND)
I have _____ to give my boss a piece of my mind and then hand in my notice.

303. Havoc followed directly as a consequence of the tornadoes that swept across the country. (WAKE)
Havoc followed _____ the tornadoes that swept across the country.

304. Curfew has been declared by the authorities because of the recent terrorist threats. (OWING)
Authorities have _____ the recent terrorist threats.

305. The newspaper reviewers are levelling heavy criticism at the writer's new book. (**COMING**)
The newspaper reviewers are _____
_____ new book.

306. Old-fashioned as their ideas may sound, they are valid to this day. (**HOLD**)
Their ideas may seem old-fashioned, but they _____
_____ to this day.

307. Susan and her mother stopped being friends because of a pointless argument and haven't spoken to each other ever since. (**FALLEN**)
Susan and her mother _____
a pointless argument and haven't spoken to each other ever since.

308. We wanted to continue our tour of the city centre but the weather didn't permit it. (**LIKE**)
We _____ on with our tour of the city centre but the weather didn't permit it.

309. This mystery is still waiting for an explanation. (**REMAINS**)
There _____ still waiting for an explanation.

310. It would be difficult for Laura to pay for all her expenses without the help of her friends. (**ENDS**)
Laura would have a lot of _____
it weren't for the help of her friends.

311. I was most surprised to run into Adam at the party. (**VERY**)
Adam was _____ I'd expect to meet at the party.

312. It surprised me to learn that John stopped smoking because he wanted to improve his health. (**SURPRISE**)
Much _____ up smoking because he wanted to improve his health.

313. My adviser says she's been too busy to start marking my paper but promised she would do that as soon as possible. (**DOWN**)
My adviser says she _____ my paper yet but promised she would do that as soon as possible.

314. As a young adult, he still behaves like he used to in his teenage years. (**MUCH**)
As a young adult, he still behaves _____ as he did in his teenage years.

315. Sandra's offensive remarks make her mother angry, which is perfectly understandable. (**BLAME**)
Sandra's _____ getting angry at her daughter's offensive remarks.

316. My boss only ever criticized my work and never really appreciated me. (**FAULT**)
My boss was forever _____ my work and never really appreciated me.

317. I've had the intention of replying to your email, but I haven't yet had any time to do so. (**MEANING**)
Though I _____, I haven't yet had any time to reply to your email.

318. My old car is not working well. It just won't start. (**PLAYING**)
My old car _____ up. It just won't start.

319. I'm not really sure, but I think they've broken up. (**KNOWLEDGE**)
To _____, they've broken up.

320. I moved to France because I was deeply fascinated by this country. (**MUCH**)
I was deeply fascinated by France, so _____ _____ I moved to this country.

321. If you take your medicine as the doctor prescribed, you will recover very quickly. (**TIME**)
If you take our medicine as the doctor prescribed, you will recover in _____ all.

322. All the prisoners have to answer for their actions in case of misbehaviour. (**ANSWERABLE**)
All the prisoners must _____ for their actions in case of misbehaviour.

323. In next to no time, I'm sure you'll take to your new co-workers. (**LIKING**)
In next to no time, I'm sure you'll _____ your new co-workers.

324. My brother was rude to me but I got my revenge on him. (**BACK**)
I paid _____ rude to me.

325. We definitely can't get this done in time. (**WAY**)
There is _____ to get this done in time.

END OF C1. GO ON TO C2 (PROFICIENCY) ➡ ➡ ➡ ➡ ➡ ➡

KWT 326 to 500

REVISE FOR CAMBRIDGE UNIVERSITY CERTIFICATES OF ENGLISH

PROFICIENCY (C2)

Complete the second sentence so that it has a similar meaning to the first sentence, as in the example.

➡ You <u>must</u> use between **3** and **8** words.
➡ Do <u>not</u> change the key word in any way. (given in brackets, capital letters, bold type).
➡ Short forms (*isn't, don't, didn't, won't, couldn't...* etc.) count as two words (you may use either one) The genitive (*Peter's, children's, today's...* etc.) counts as one word only.

Example:

He is unhappy because he didn't get a promotion at work. (**DUMPS**)
He's _____ he didn't get a promotion at work.
Answer key ➥ He's *(been) **down in the dumps** because* he didn't get a promotion at work.

326. She was determined to pass the final examinations. (**SET**)
She was dead _____ the final examinations.

327. As soon as I got into the bathtub, I heard someone knocking on the door. (**SOONER**)
No _____ I heard someone knocking on the door.

328. I was not sure if I wanted to stay. (**MINDS**)
I _____ to stay.

329. It took me a lot of time to find out what my condition was. (**DID**)
Only after a lot of time _____ what my condition was.

330. Her first flight experience was a nightmare, but this didn't harm her at all. (**WORSE**)
Her first flight was a nightmare, but she _____ _____ this experience.

331. They say a visual presentation is more efficient than words. (**PAINTS**)
As the saying goes, 'A _____ words'.

332. He was offended that his teacher called him a nuisance. (**OFFENCE**)
He took _____ his teacher.

333. She was slowly accepting the death of her cat. (**TERMS**)
She was slowly _____ her cat had died.

334. He was offended by his teacher's accusations that he had cheated in the exam. (**EXCEPTION**)
He _____ of cheating in the exam.

335. 'I would prefer to stay in, if you don't mind,' he told her. (**SOON**)
'I would _____ stay in, if you don't mind,' he told her.

336. Thank goodness you didn't come to the party. It was awful. (**WELL**)
It _____ you didn't come to the party. It was awful.

337. He mistakenly believes his mother will always be at his beck and call. (**GRANTED**)
He _____ his mother will always be at his beck and call.

338. I have read the instructions carefully, but I haven't understood them at all. (**NONE**)
I have read the instructions carefully, but I'm _____ _____ wiser.

339. Ann just couldn't imagine what she was in for. (**DID**)
Little _____ what she was in for.

340. 'Would you like to go away at the weekend?' he asked me. (**MOOD**)
He asked me _____ away at the weekend.

341. Peter was exhausted and also had a nasty cold. (**ONLY**)
Not _____ had a nasty cold.

342. Do you mind if I watch TV while you're reading? (**OBJECTION**)
Do you _____ TV while you're reading?

343. His cold heart was completely devoid of feelings. (**WHATSOEVER**)
There were _____ in his cold heart.

344. It is difficult to predict how long it will take for him to recover. (**TELLING**)
There _____ take.

345. For me, her skill as an actress was most impressive. (**HOW**)
I was _____ was.

346. Everybody expected the politician to resign, so no one was surprised. (**CAME**)
The politician's _____ anyone.

347. Everyone was surprised that the politician had resigned. (**SURPRISE**)
The politician had resigned, which _____
_____ everyone.

348. When she was at her most successful, the princess enjoyed enormous popularity. (**HEIGHT**)
At _____, the princess enjoyed enormous popularity.

349. Although we were worried, it wasn't necessary because they had already come up with a solution. (**NEEDN'T**)
We _____ because they had already come up with a solution.

350. I warned her not to be remiss in her duties, but I had no success. (**WAS**)
I warned her not to be remiss in her duties, but _____ _____ avail.

351. 'Were you satisfied with the service, sir?' the waiter asked. (**LIKING**)
The waiter asked, 'Was _____, sir?'

352. He had the audacity, without any evidence, to accuse me of involvement in the fraudulent scheme. (**FAR**)
He went _____ involved in the fraudulent scheme.

353. It was highly probable that Glenn would become an acclaimed actress. (**MAKINGS**)
Glenn had _____ an acclaimed actress.

354. Sandra is by far the best student in her class. (**ANYWHERE**)
There is no _____ Sandra in her class.

355. Mark is far superior to me in terms of grammar knowledge. (**MATCH**)
When it _____ for Mark.

356. The committee decided to postpone the examination, which was welcomed by all the candidates. (**DECISION**)
The committee's _____ all the candidates.

357. If you study very hard, the content won't be so difficult. (**EASIER**)
The _____ the content will be.

358. The stranded cat would never have been rescued if the rescuer hadn't come up with an ingenious plan. (**INGENUITY**)
But _____ plan, the stranded cat would never have been rescued.

359. Besides making you fit, there are many other reasons why you should do physical exercise. (**MORE**)
There _____ getting fit.

360. The teacher got angry with his students and started shouting at them. (**TEMPER**)
The teacher _____ with the students and started shouting at them.

361. They still haven't found out what caused the disaster. (**CAUSE**)
They have yet _____ the disaster was.

362. Three actresses were competing for the leading role in the musical. (**CONTENTION**)
There _____ the leading role in the musical.

363. The spokesman for the government said that the information was mere conjecture. (**DISMISSED**)
The information _____ than conjecture by the government's spokesman.

364. Danny wasn't at all disheartened by that unpleasant experience. (**PUT**)
That unpleasant experience didn't _____ least.

365. Paul has hinted that he doesn't wish to remain in the company any longer. (**HINT**)
Paul has dropped _____ wishes to remain in the company.

366. He was immersed in his reading, in such a way that he didn't notice when the telephone rang. (**WRAPPED**)
He was so _____ didn't notice when the telephone rang.

367. The ballet school is always looking for new talents. (**LOOKOUT**)
The ballet school is always _____ new talents.

368. How does Anne earn a living? (**DO**)
What _____ a living?

369. I'd say, in less forceful words, the students are a bit lively. (**PUT**)
The students are a bit lively, _____ mildly.

370. I don't know why Tina made such a controversial decision. (**PROMPTED**)
I don't know _____ a decision.

371. I tried to be like one of my idols when I was a young teacher. (**MODELLED**)
As _____ of my idols.

372. The team planned everything as carefully as they could possibly have done. (**UTMOST**)
Everything _____ by the team.

373. I promised them that such an embarrassing situation would never be repeated. (**WORD**)
I gave _____ repetition of such an embarrassing situation.

374. Coming second didn't make him feel any better because what Paul really wanted was win. (**CONSOLATION**)
Coming second _____ was all that Paul cared about.

375. Jack finds that sometimes watching movies helps him stop thinking about his schoolwork. (**MIND**)
Jack finds that sometimes watching movies helps him _____ _____ his schoolwork.

376. I made an effort not to get involved in that awkward situation. (**MIXED**)
I tried hard to keep _____ that awkward situation.

377. He announced that he would resign, and then said he had not been involved in the crime. (**WENT**)
After announcing his _____ been involved in the crime.

378. She realized that she was in a delicate situation and wasn't to blame for it. (**FAULT**)
Through _____ herself in a delicate situation.

379. I'm doubtful that this objective is really attainable. (**RESERVATIONS**)
I have _____ this objective really is.

380. Francesca chose marketing rather than computing for her summer course. (**PREFERENCE**)
Francesca opted _____ for her summer course.

381. I'd say you should practise eight hours a day. (**THUMB**)
As _____, you should practice eight hours a day.

382. The demonstrators demanded that the government should ban animal experiments in the cosmetics industry. (**EXPERIMENTING**)
The demonstrators called _____ animals in the cosmetics industry.

383. 'I don't like how touristy Venice has become,' she said. (**LIKING**)
'Venice has become _____,' she said.

384. Needles to say, I'm forever indebted to you for your support. (**SAYING**)
It goes _____ I'm forever indebted to you for your support.

385. This event wouldn't have been possible without your unwavering support. (**MADE**)
Your unwavering support was _____ to take place.

386. It's a pity the trainer made us believe that we were doing well, when we weren't. (**LED**)
If only _____ that we were doing well, when we weren't.

387. Disrespect is something that is not possible for me to tolerate. (**PUT**)
I find _____ disrespect.

388. Even though the exercise may be hard, it helps to get your body into shape. (**AS**)
Hard _____, it helps to get your body into shape.

389. I suddenly realised that I was making an unwise decision. (**DAWNED**)
Suddenly _____ that I was making an unwise decision.

390. At first I didn't want to go, but in the end I changed my mind. (**HEART**)
At first I didn't want to go, but in the end I _____ _____ and decided to go.

391. His menial job has never been an ordeal for him. (**REGARDED**)
His menial job _____ an ordeal by him.

68

392. University professors tend to feel superior to secondary school teachers. (**LOOK**)
University professors have a _____
on secondary school teachers.

393. Let's go home. I don't feel comfortable at all at this party. (**PLACE**)
Let's go home. I feel _____ at this party.

394. The girls were shocked to find out that Brad had stolen their money. (**MADE**)
The girls were shocked to find out that Brad _____
_____ their money.

395. We should always be grateful for what we're given for free, shouldn't we? (**HORSE**)
We should _____ the mouth, should we?

396. In regards to fashion, he is a very discerning customer. (**DOWN**)
When it _____ fashion, he is a very discerning customer.

397. You shouldn't worry about other people's safety while sacrificing your own. (**EXPENSE**)
You shouldn't worry about other people's safety _____
_____ own.

398. 'No matter what happens, I won't step down,' the president said. (**MAY**)
The president said, '_____, I won't step down.'

399. He almost admitted that he had lied before the judge. (**MUCH**)
He _____ admitted that he had lied before the judge.

400. 'The students' behaviour was nothing less than obnoxious,' the teacher said. (**SHORT**)
The teacher said, 'The students' behaviour was _____ _____ obnoxious.'

401. Even though I hold him in high regard, I have to disagree with him on this complicated matter. (**MUCH**)
As _____, I have to disagree with him on this complicated matter.

402. 'Only you can sign this document,' my secretary told me. (**OTHER**)
My secretary said that the document _____ me.

403. In your opinion, does he have all the necessary qualifications to be in charge of the academic department? (**TAKES**)
Do you think _____ in charge of the academic department?

404. The student stupidly started shouting at her teacher. (**HEAD**)
The student went _____ and started shouting at her teacher.

405. At the movie conference, I had the tremendous opportunity to meet the Meryl Streep in the flesh. (**NONE**)
At the movie conference, I met _____ the Meryl Streep in the flesh.

406. I always try to be hopeful, even if things will sometimes go off track. (**SIDE**)
I always try to look _____ even if things will sometimes go off track.

407. The student's success will depend basically on her commitment to her duties. (**MORE**)
Basically, the more _____ the student will be.

408. The twins are completely different from each other. (**RESEMBLANCE**)
The twins bear _____ each other.

409. The cats don't feel uncomfortable at all when the mastiff is around. (**EASE**)
The cats feel _____ the mastiff around.

410. The student has a better attitude to school now that his teacher has spoken to him. (**IMPROVED**)
The student's attitude to school has _____ his teacher.

411. He may seem a little bashful at first sight, but looks can be deceptive. (**OFF**)
He may _____ a little bashful at first sight, but looks can be deceptive.

412. If this tense situation escalates, we'll have to call the police. (**COMES**)
If worse _____, we'll have to call the police.

413. 'Have you forgotten everything about the accident?' she asked me. (**RECOLLECTION**)
She asked me, 'Don't _____ the accident?'

414. It was so inappropriate of you to yell at your mother like that. (**ORDER**)
You _____ to yell at your mother like that.

415. It is definitely not possible for me to ask her for support. (**QUESTION**)
Asking _____ for me.

416. He asked me, 'Do you think I should go ahead with the project?' (**ADVISABLE**)
He asked me if _____ ahead with the project.

417. The teacher was very competent, and approachable too. (**ONLY**)
Not _____ approachable.

418. Peter showed deep regret, as he should have. (**WELL**)
Peter was deeply _____ might.

419. Since the concert has been called off, it would be better if we stayed at home. (**MAY**)
We _____ at home, since the concert has been called off.

420. You were lucky not to have come. The party is awfully boring. (**WELL**)
It is just _____ come. The party is awfully boring.

421. I told you it was a waste of time to try to make him study harder. (**POINTLESS**)
I told you it would _____ to make him study harder.

422. 'I wish you would stop making fun of me,' she shouted. (**JOKES**)
She shouted, 'Stop _____ expense, will you?'

423. You can trust him with confidential information. He always keeps his promises. (**WORD**)
He is as _____, so you can trust him with confidential information.

424. Surely you agree with me that the Nobel laureate composes with flair? (**WAY**)
Surely you agree with me that the Noel laureate _____ _____ words?

72

425. I wasn't expecting at all that you would stand up to the boss at the meeting. (**ABACK**)
I _____ up to the boss at the meeting.

426. Robert usually writes excellent compositions, but this one is a bit disappointing. (**MAIN**)
Robert writes excellent compositions _____
_____, but this one is a bit disappointing.

427. They wouldn't have rescued you without the help of the police dogs. (**HAD**)
Never would _____ been for the help of the police dogs.

428. Apart from being a F1 champion, he was also very congenial. (**WELL**)
As _____ a Formula 1 champion, he was also very congenial.

429. The students were told to either keep quiet or leave the classroom. (**NO**)
The students were _____ keep quiet or leave the classroom.

430. Shortly after I opened the door, a car pulled up near my house. (**WHEN**)
Scarcely _____ a car pulled up near my house.

431. 'Don't you think you should start behaving like an adult?' my father said. (**THOUGH**)
My father said, 'It's high _____ not an adult.'

432. Have you ever attempted to write a book? (**GO**)
Have you ever _____ writing a book?

433. Surely the local papers treated the problem far too seriously? (**PROPORTION**)
Don't you think the problem _____ the local papers?

434. People believed that the scientist's discovery would unravel the mysteries of the universe. (**BARE**)
It was _____ the mysteries of the universe.

435. Would someone please tell me what's happening here? (**LET**)
Would someone please _____ on what's happening here?

436. 'I'll stand by you, whatever happens!' she promised me. (**THICK**)
She promised me she would stick _____ thin.

437. My phone was low on battery, but the passenger sitting next to me lent me his charger. (**LUCK**)
My phone was low on battery but, as _____ it, the passenger sitting next to me lent me his charger.

438. Who could possibly have imagined that I would inherit anything? (**THOUGHT**)
Who would _____ into an inheritance?

439. Were Iguaçu Falls what you expected? (**LIVE**)
Did _____ expectations?

440. We got to the train station just on time. (**NICK**)
We got to the train station just _____ time.

441. Would you like to eat anything? (**CARE**)
Would you _____ eat?

442. A life of hardship will be of no benefit to us. (**DO**)
I life of hardship _____ good.

443. They say strict discipline at school is beneficial for character building. (**WONDERS**)
It is _____ for character building.

444. Could you help me carry this heavy box? (**TURN**)
Could you _____ me carry this heavy box?

445. I'm tired of all the hard work around here. (**DONKEY**)
I'm fed _____ around here.

446. Benefiting from what I know now, it's easy to say that quitting was wrong. (**HINDSIGHT**)
With the _____, it's easy to say that quitting was wrong.

447. Machado's novels are the most extraordinary I've ever read. (**ONE**)
I've yet _____ Machado's.

448. She has not been seen for two days. (**SIGHT**)
No one _____ for two days.

449. They felt the candidate didn't meet the standards required. (**HAVE**)
The candidate was _____ the standards required.

450. They didn't tell her what she should do, so she did it her own way. (**BEEN**)
Not _____ what she should do, she did it her own way.

451. Never before have I taught students who are so well-behaved. (**SUCH**)
This is _____ well-behaved students.

452. The idea was originally to publish the book by October at the latest. (**DUE**)
The book _____ by October at the latest.

453. It appears that the clients have received false information. (**GIVEN**)
The clients _____ false information.

454. I want it to be clear to my students that I'm a tough teacher, but I'm fair. (**SEEN**)
I want to _____ who's tough, but fair.

455. It looks as though he has made a mistake filling in his form. (**FILLED**)
He seems to _____ incorrectly.

456. She called in sick, so someone else had to substitute for her. (**FILL**)
Since she had _____ in for her.

457. I did not hesitate to lie because I was just trying to help a friend. (**QUALMS**)
I have _____ lied because I was just trying to help a friend.

458. 'Please refrain from interrupting me while I'm explaining the content,' the teacher said. (**BUTTING**)
The teacher said, 'I wish _____ while I'm explaining the content.'

459. The officer's report and the defendant's version didn't add up. (**ODDS**)
The defendant's version _____ the officer's report.

460. Her friends regarded her so highly that she had everyone's unflagging support. (**HELD**)
Such _____ by her friends that she had everyone's unflagging support.

461. There were thousands of angry demonstrators on the streets. (**PACKED**)
The streets _____ angry demonstrators.

462. My passport was stolen when I was abroad. (**ROBBED**)
I _____ my passport when I was abroad.

463. The president has been given an honorary doctorate by Sorbonne university. (**CONFERRED**)
An honorary degree by Sorbonne university _____ _____ the president.

464. They believe a fault in one of the engines was behind the accident. (**BROUGHT**)
A fault in one of the engines _____ the accident.

465. The local people referred to the nurse as 'The Angel of Death'. (**DUBBED**)
The _____ 'The Angel of Death' by the local people.

466. The candidate finally took the presidential oath. (**SWORN**)
The candidate _____ president.

467. It's just possible that the students may need extra time. (**RULED**)
The possibility of _____ out.

468. You're not supposed to leave the examination room unless the proctors direct you to do so. (**ARE**)
You are only _____ directed to do so by the proctors.

469. I can't find my glasses. I know! I suppose I accidentally left them at the office. (**THINK**)
I can't find my glasses. Come _____ it, I accidentally left them at the office.

470. The examination was shorter, but in fact it was more difficult than usual. (**RATE**)
The examination was shorter, but _____
it was more difficult than usual.

471. He made a commitment to give up drinking alcohol. (**ABSTAIN**)
He took _____ alcohol.

472. If the employees involved make one more mistake, they will be dismissed. (**DISMISSAL**)
One more mistake will lead _____
involved.

473. I reject the biased notion that some people are superior to others. (**SUBSCRIBE**)
I _____ the biased notion
that some people are superior to others.

474. Hawking was something of a legend, so to speak, someone all aspiring scholars wanted to be. (**WERE**)
Hawking was something of a legend, _____
_____, someone all aspiring scholars wanted to be.

475. As we drove round the corner, we couldn't see the old mansion any more. (**WENT**)
As we drove round the corner, the old mansion _____
_____ sight.

476. We need at least five people. If more people want to participate, we'll be happy, though. (**MORE**)
We need at least five people, _____
merrier.

477. 'Please don't go far, so I can see you,' the counselor told the children. (**SIGHT**)
'Children, don't go _____ you?' the
counselor warned them.

478. When travelling abroad, you can't take it for granted that everything will go smoothly. (**ALLOWANCE**)
When travelling abroad, you have _____ mishaps.

479. The prisoner, who was on parole, completely disappeared. (**VANISHED**)
The prisoner, who was on parole, _____ air.

480. 'In a war, while we're fighting relentlessly, who can tell who's right or wrong?' he asked us. (**THICK**)
'In a war, _____ fight, who can tell who's right or wrong?' he asked us.

481. Sometimes you have to turn a blind eye to your father's cantankerousness; after all, he's at an advanced age. (**ALLOWANCE**)
Since he's at an advanced age, sometimes you have _____ _____ cantankerousness.

482. Sometimes I don't believe what he says completely. (**PINCH**)
Sometimes I take _____ salt.

483. It was uncertain that she would pass her driving test. (**TOUCH**)
It _____ not she'd pass her driving test.

484. Don't you think this is a storm in a teacup? (**FUSS**)
Don't you think you're _____ something unimportant?

485. To Tina, Ayrton was simply the best in his field. (**NONE**)
To Tina, Ayrton was _____ in his field.

486. John looks exactly like his father. (**SPITTING**)
John _____ his father.

487. I think you were trying something very difficult, considering your inexperience. (**BITE**)
I think you were trying to _____ chew, considering your inexperience.

488. His discouraging words dampened my enthusiasm, so I gave it all up. (**BLOW**)
His discouraging words _____ my enthusiasm, so I gave it all up.

489. Years on end of not eating healthily have begun to affect her. (**TOLL**)
Years on end of not eating healthily have begun _____ her.

490. Shouldn't we think about those who are less fortunate than ourselves? (**SPARE**)
Shouldn't we _____ those who are less fortunate than ourselves?

491. Either you learn not to act too proud, or you'll get yourself into trouble at school. (**HEAD**)
Either your learn to keep _____, or you'll get yourself into trouble at school.

492. If you're serious about getting into university, you'd better organize your studies more effectively. (**ACT**)
You'd better get _____ if you're serious about getting into university.

493. I'm not collecting money for myself, but for charity. (**OWN**)
I'm collecting money _____ behalf.

494. It would be wiser to walk into town instead of driving, as there's too much traffic now. (**OFF**)
You'd _____ into town, as there's too much traffic now.

495. I cannot understand why Sheila divorced her husband in the first place. (**BEYOND**)
Why Sheila divorced her husband _____ me.

496. You wouldn't mind posting this for me, would you? (**NO**)
Could you possibly _____ bother?

497. We apologize for the inconvenience. Please accept this upgrade from the airline for free. (**AIRLINE'S**)
We apologize for the inconvenience. Please accept this upgrade _____ compliments.

498. I sometimes travel abroad on holiday. (**THEN**)
Every _____ I travel abroad on holiday.

499. Her desk is a mess, so she deserves it if she never finds anything. (**SERVES**)
Her desk is a mess, so _____
she never finds anything.

500. Alcohol addiction almost destroyed her professional career. (**BUT**)
Her career _____ by alcohol addiction.

END OF C2 (PROFICIENCY)

ANSWER KEY

FIRST (B2)

1. The plane took off before I got to the airport. (**ALREADY**) → When I got to the airport, the plane **had already taken** off.

Note(s): When an aircraft *takes off*, it leaves the ground. Figuratively, we can also say that a business takes off (that is, becomes successful). (Near-)synonym(s) of *take off* include(s): *depart, lift off, soar*, etc. Opposite(s): *arrive, land, come in*, etc.

2. I didn't understand what he said because he spoke very fast. (**TOO**) → He spoke **too fast for me to** understand what he said.

3. He will never come here again. (**LAST**) → This is the **last time he has come** here.

Note(s): We always use the **present perfect** in structures such as *This is the first/second... last time (that)...* Therefore, "This is the first/last time I come/ am coming..." are incorrect.

4. Do you think you can convince him to take part in the scheme? (**INTO**) → Do you think you can talk **him into taking** part in the scheme?

5. I persuaded her not to take part in the fraudulent scheme. (**OUT**) → I **talked her out of taking** part in the fraudulent scheme.

Note(s): Note these formal (near-) synonyms of *talk into/out*: *convince, persuade* (into), *discourage, dissuade* (out), etc. Related word(s): *convincement, persuasion, discouragement, dissuasion* (**nouns**).

6. I bought this car two years ago. (**HAD**) → I **have had this car for** two years.

Note(s): We use the **past simple** in the lead-in because it says exactly when something started (*two years ago*), while in the answer we focus on duration up to now (we look at the action simultaneously in the past and the present).

7. I'm dying to go on a tour of Brazil. (**FORWARD**) → I am *looking forward to going* on a tour of Brazil.

Note(s): A potential mistake here is using the **infinitive** after *to*. ("... looking forward to go"). We use the **gerund** because in *looking forward to* something, *to* is a **preposition**. Take note of these (near-) synonyms: *to crave, to yearn, to set you heart on*.

8. When she was younger, Ann didn't like to read. (**USE**) → Ann *did not use to read* when she was younger.

Note(s): Use the **verb** in the **infinitive** without *to*, as is the case with all other English verbs whose **past** is formed with the **auxiliary** *did*. "Ann did not ~~used~~ to read..." is a very common mistake.

9. I've had English classes since the beginning of the year. (**STUDYING**) → I *have been studying* English since the beginning of the year.

10. I've never tried snails before. (**HAVE**) → This is the first time I *have ever tried/eaten* snails.

11. Danny spoke to Paula, and then she found out he had had an accident. (**UNTIL**) → Paula didn't find out Danny had *had an accident until he* spoke to her.

Note(s): In the lead-in, where you read "... found out he *had had* an accident", the **past perfect** is optional (the **simple past** will suffice here: "... found out he *had* an accident) because *and then* establishes the order of the events.

12. She really regrets not having enrolled for the examination. (**WISHES**) → She *wishes she had enrolled* for the examination.

Note(s): Note that the lead-in can be rephrased as: "She really regrets not enrolling...". The **gerund** alone is enough to convey the idea of past action.

13. John decided to go to bed because he was utterly exhausted. (**THAT**) → John was *so exhausted that* he decided to go to bed.

Note(s): In the lead-in, we have the **non-gradable adjective** *exhausted*; as such, it does not collocate with *very* or *extremely*. Some useful collocations instead, include: *absolutely, completely, thoroughly, totally*, etc.

14. I kept trying, but I knew it was no use. (**EVEN**) → I kept trying, *even though* I knew it was no use.

15. 'Well done for passing your finals, Susan', said her teacher. (**CONGRATULATED**) → Susan *was congratulated on passing her* finals by her teacher.

16. 'I didn't help you because you lied to me,' he said. (**HELPED**) → 'I *could/might/would have helped you if* you hadn't lied to me,' he said.

Note(s): Using *would* (instead of *could* or *might*) conveys more certainty.

17. If you had told me, I might have been able to help you. (**ONLY**) → If *only you had* told me, I might have been able to help you.

18. This is the first time Richard has visited Brazil. (**VISIT**) → This is Richard's *first visit* to Brazil.

19. Sandra and Paul were arguing fiercely when I arrived. (**ARGUMENT**) → Sandra was *having a fierce argument with* Paul when I arrived.

Note(s): Also note these interesting **adjectives** which collocate with *argument*, conveying the same meaning: *bitter, furious* and *heated*. (Near-)synonym(s) of *argument*: *altercation, quarrel, row*, etc. Related word(s): *argumentative* (that is, *belligerent, confrontational, opinionated, pugnacious, quarrelsome*, etc.).

20. Those children's parents live near me. (**WHOSE**) → Those are *the children whose parents* live near me.

21. Given the circumstances, the only thing we could do was help. (**BUT**) → We had *no choice/alternative/option but to* help.

22. My motorbike is in very bad condition, so it won't last much longer. (**SUCH**) → My motorbike is *in such bad condition that* it won't last much longer.

<u>Note(s)</u>: As used above, *condition* is an **uncountable noun**, therefore we cannot use *a* before it ("... in such a~~ bad condition...").

23. It was careless of us to leave without closing the windows. (**SHOULD**) → We *should have closed* the windows before we left.

24. If the sun is shining, we're going to the beach at the weekend. (**UNLESS**) → We're going to the beach at the weekend, *unless the sun is not* shining.

25. We're going to the beach, unless it is raining. (**NOT**) → We're going to the beach if *it is not* raining.

26. Do you have any plans for the weekend? (**GOING**) → What *are you going to do* at the weekend?

<u>Note(s)</u>: We do not usually use *will* to ask what someone intends to do in the near future. The answer could be rephrased with the **future continuous**, as "What *will* you *be doing*...?" (close in meaning) or the **present continuous**, as "What *are* you *doing*...", when we believe the person already has an arrangement and has no intention of changing it.

27. We will get to the cinema after the beginning of the film. (**HAVE**) → By the time we get to the cinema, *the film will already have* begun.

<u>Note(s)</u>: or: "... will have *already*..." (notice the position of *already*).

28. 'Does this bus go to the university?' (**GOES**) → Could you tell me *if this bus goes* to the university?

29. He said, 'I'll give you a lift to work.' (**ME**) → He said he *would give me* a lift to work.

30. 'That's false! I've never been expelled from school,' said Tina. (**HAVING**) → Tina denied *having ever been expelled* from school.

Note(s): As pointed out before, the gerund alone can convey past idea: "Tina denied ever *being* expelled...".

31. We haven't been to the cinema for ages. (**SINCE**) → It's ages *since we last went* to the cinema.

32. The last time I was in Paris was in 2015. (**BEEN**) → I *have not been to* Paris since 2015.

33. This is my first experience as an air traveller. (**NEVER**) → I *have never travelled* by plane before.

Note(s): Be careful about the different spelling in British and American English: travel (trave*ll*ing, trave*ll*ed, trave*ll*er); in *AmE.*, these words are usually spelled with one 'l' only.

34. When did they start to go out together? (**GOING**) → How *long have they been going* out together?

35. I will have to manage without taking a holiday abroad this year. (**DO**) → I will have to *(make) do without* a holiday abroad this year.

36. I haven't found time to answer your e-mail yet. (**ROUND**) → I still haven't *got round to answering* your e-mail yet.

37. The hotel's service was atrocious, but the meals were sumptuous. (**MADE**) → The hotel's sumptuous meals *made up for* its atrocious service.

Note(s): You've probably noticed the words *atrocious* and *sumptuous*. Also note these collocations for *service* and *meals*: bad, poor and terrible service (**adjectives**); *lavish* meal (**adjective**).

38. 'I'm afraid I'm a bit indisposed to go out, Sally,' answered Joe. (**UP**) → Joe told sally he was ***not feeling up to going*** out.

39. After working hard, I was eager to have a substantial meal. (**MOOD**)
→ After working hard, I was *in the mood for* a substantial meal.

Note(s): You can also say that a *substantial* meal is a *square* meal (collocation patterns).

40. You should've already learned to defend yourself by now. (**STAND**)
→ It's high time you *learned to stand up for* yourself.

41. On my way back home from work, I paid a friend a short visit. (**CALLED**) → I *called on* a friend on my way back home from work.

42. I almost never get the recognition I think I deserve. (**DO**) → Seldom *do I get* the recognition I think I deserve.

43. I realised only then that I had lost my wallet. (**REALISE**) → Only then *did I realise* that I had lost my wallet.

Note(s): Note this **noun** related to the **verb** *to realise*: "The *realisation* dawned (on me) that I would never get the promotion" (= awareness).

44. Never forget to close the windows under any circumstances. (**SHOULD**)
→ Under *no circumstances should you forget* to close the windows.

45. 'I will not tolerate your unacceptable behaviour any longer,' my father said to me. (**PUT**) → My father said to me that he would *no longer put up with* my unacceptable behaviour.

46. We don't have much time left, so we'd better work faster. (**RUNNING**)
→ We'd better work faster because we're *running out/short of* time.

47. The student didn't once offer his teacher a word of apology. (**OFFER**)
→ Not *once did the student offer* his teacher a word of apology.

48. Putting myself in your situation, I'd look for medical help. (**WERE**)
→ If *I were you*, I'd look for medical help.

Note(s): *Was* would be colloquial: "If I *was* you, I'd look for...". It may be accepted, depending on the context.

49. Under no circumstances should this door be opened during the flight. (**NOT**) → This door should **not be opened under any** circumstances during the flight.

50. Have you thought of a solution to the problem yet? (**COME**) → Have you **come up with** a solution to the problem yet?

51. If the weather isn't favourable, we'll cancel the match. (**OFF**) → If the weather isn't favourable, we'll **call off** the match.

Note(s): Or: "... *call* the match *off*" (*To call off* is a separable phrasal verb).

52. I'll give you a guided tour of the city, what do you think? (**AROUND**) → Shall *I show you around* the city?

53. How about postponing the meeting until next week? (**PUTTING**) → How about *putting off the meeting* until next week?

Note(s): 1) This is a separable phrasal verb (or: "... *putting* the meeting *off*...?") 2) It can be followed by a verb ("I can't putt off *seeing* the doctor any longer.") 3) Also note this meaning (*discourage*): "Her smell of cigarette puts me off" (that is, makes me lose interest in her).

54. 'Keep our secret to yourself, will you?' Susan asked her friend. (**GIVE**) → Susan asked her friend *not to give their secret* away.

55. I think Joe has eaten less chocolate because he's much fitter now. (**CUT**) → Joe *must have cut down on* chocolate because he's much fitter now.

56. My teacher suggested I should study languages to enhance my memory. (**ADVISED**) → I *was advised to study* languages to enhance my memory by my teacher.

<u>Note(s)</u>: It is worth studying these patterns of *advise*: it can be followed by either 1) an **object** + **infinitive** with *to* "The teacher advised <u>me to study</u> harder" 2) or followed by the **gerund**, without **object**: "The teacher advised studying harder". Also note this construction: "The teacher advised <u>against</u> cheat*ing* in the exams". Related word(s): *advisory*, *advisable* (**adjectives**); *advisability* (**noun**).

57. The novel was so exciting that I just couldn't put it down. (**SUCH**) → It <u>was such an exciting novel</u> that I just couldn't put it down.

<u>Note(s)</u>: Such exciting reading can be referred to as *unputdownable* (**adjective**).

58. Students quite often arrive late. (**COMMON**) → It <u>is not common for students</u> to arrive early.

59. Henry doesn't find it strange to work in groups any more. (**USED**) → Henry has <u>got used to working</u> in groups now.

60. I'm looking forward to going on holiday. (**DYING**) → I <u>am dying to go</u> on holiday.

61. Studying hard is a new experience for her. (**USED**) → She has <u>not got used to studying</u> hard yet.

62. Did she study hard when she was at university? (**USE**) → Did <u>she use to study</u> hard when she was at university?

63. Jane always found it difficult to give her students a scold. (**USED**) → Jane just couldn't <u>get used to giving</u> her students a scold.

64. I badly need a holiday. I'm completely worn out. (**DO**) → I could <u>do with</u> a holiday. I'm completely worn out.

65. They had their house redecorated, and then moved in. (**UP**) → They <u>got/had their house done up</u>, and then moved in.

66. The government has promised to abolish capital punishment. (**AWAY**) → The government has promised to *do away with* capital punishment.

Note(s): 1) Take note of this formal (near-) synonym of *do away with* and its related word(s): to abolish; *abolishable* (**adjective**), *abolishment* (**noun**). Opposite(s): *to enforce*. 2) *To do away with* someone means *to kill*.

67. I don't usually go out at weekends. (**UNUSUAL**) → It is *unusual for me to go* out at weekends.

68. When I was a kid, I usually walked to school. (**WOULD**) → When I was a kid, I *would usually walk* to school.

Note(s): When we use *would* to talk about the past, it is close in meaning to *used to*, as in "... When I was a kid, I usually *used to* walk to school".

69. Before then, the children had never had to put their toys away. (**EVER**) → That was the first time the children *had ever had* to put their toys away.

Note(s): If you *put something away*, you put it where it is usually kept.

70. How long will it be before you've finished your homework? (**TAKE**) → How long *will it take (for) you* to finish your homework?

71. I'm finding it difficult to get all my work done punctually. (**DIFFICULTY**) → I *am having difficulty (in) getting* all my work done punctually.

72. I have never read a better book than this one. (**FAR**) → This *by far the best book* I have read.

73. 'The manager will investigate your complaints as soon as possible,' the receptionist told me. (**LOOKED**) → I was told by the receptionist that my complaints *would be looked into by* the manager as soon as possible.

74. Last year, unfavourable weather conditions caused the postponement of the championship. (**BECAUSE**) → Last year, the championship *was postponed because of* unfavourable weather conditions.

Note(s): 1) Here are some words we can use to talk about bad, unfavourable weather: *adverse, atrocious, awful, inclement*. 2) Remember that *to put off* means the same as *to postpone*, depending on the context.

75. Jonh does not want to continue to work for this company any more. (**CARRY**) → John no *longer wants to carry on* working for this company.

76. The rate of crime has not increased so far this year. (**INCREASE**) → There *has been no increase in* the rate of crime so far this year.

Note(s): As a **noun**, *increase* is followed by the **preposition** *in*; as a **verb**, it is followed by *to*.

77. I cannot get all my suitcases into the baggage compartment. (**BIG**) → The baggage compartment is *not big enough to* take all my suitcases.

78. I couldn't get to school on time because of the slow traffic. (**PREVENTED**) → The slow traffic *prevented me (from) getting* to school on time.

79. He tiptoed into the house very quietly so that he wouldn't wake up anyone. (**AVOID**) → He tiptoed into the house very quietly so *as to avoid waking anyone* up.

80. Sam studied really hard so that she would get a good grade. (**ORDER**) → Sam studied really hard *in order to get* a good grade.

Note(s): Here are some useful **adjectives** we use to describe good grades: *excellent, high, top*; bad grades: *low, poor*; not good, but not too bad either: *average*. Some **verbs** which collocate with *grade* include: *to attain, to get, to obtain, to receive*, etc.

81. I think this rain has come to stay for the weekend. (**SET**) → I think this rain has *set in* for the weekend.

Note(s): *Set in* can also refer to an illness, a bed feeling, etc. "Panic *set in* when he found out what had happened to his daughter."

82. You have to fill in this form by Friday at the latest. (**FILLED**) → This form *has to/must/should be* *filled* *in* by Friday at the latest.

83. He trained very hard in order to be fit for the competition. (**WOULD**) → He trained very hard so *that he* *would* *be* fit for the competition.

84. You shouldn't eat chocolate if you're on a diet. (**OUGHT**) → You *ought* *not to eat* chocolate if you're on a diet.

85. Candidates shouldn't leave the examination room without permission. (**ALLOWED**) → Candidates *are not* *allowed* *to leave* the examination room without permission.

86. I think she should start doing physical exercise immediately. (**HAD**) → I think she *had* *better start doing* physical exercise immediately.

Note(s): "She better start..." (without *had*) is very common, but is not standard English. Do not use it in the exam.

87. 'You must leave immediately, Sarah!' said the teacher. (**HAD**) → The teacher told Sarah *(that) she* *had* *to leave* immediately.

88. Stop interrupting me, will you? It's so annoying! (**WISH**) → I *wish* *you would stop* interrupting me.

Note(s): *Wish* is usually followed by the **simple past**, as in "I wish he studied more" (he doesn't study). It is followed by *would* when we imply criticism or annoyance.

89. It wasn't necessary for us to resit the test, but we did. (**NEEDN'T**) → We *needn't* *have resat* the test, but we did.

Note(s): Maybe it's important to remember the difference: "we needn't have done" means that it was not necessary, but we did it; "we didn't need to do" means that we didn't do something because it wasn't necessary.

90. Mike is late. Perhaps he missed the bus. (**MIGHT**) → Mike is late. He *might* *have missed* the bus.

Note(s): *Could* is also possible, instead of *might*, but the latter conveys more uncertainty.

91. I was supposed to leave earlier, but that wasn't possible. (**LEFT**) → I was to *have left* earlier, but that wasn't possible.

92. I'm sure it wasn't him that you saw. He's gone to Rome on holiday. (**CAN'T**) → It *can't have been him (that/who/whom)* you saw. He's gone to Rome on holiday.

Note(s): There is an important difference between *been* and *gone* when we use the **present perfect**: "He's *been* to Rome" means that he went there and is back again; "He's *gone* to Rome" means that he hasn't come back yet.

93. I'm almost sure I've left my keys back at the office. (**MUST**) → I *must have left* my keys back at the office.

Note(s): 1) The answer can also be rephrased as: "I *may/might* have left...". *Must* implies a stronger deduction. 2) Do not use *forget* ("I must have ~~forgotten~~ my keys...") in this case.

94. Candidates are welcome to contact us if they need more information. (**TOUCH**) → 'Candidates, feel comfortable to *get in touch with* us if you need more information,' she told us.

95. I didn't buy the book because it was too expensive. (**BOUGHT**) → I *would have bought* the book if it hadn't been so expensive.

96. During the examination, I just couldn't think of the correct answer to the question. (**COME**) → During the examination, I was not *able to come up with* the correct answer to the question.

Note(s): *To come up with* is close in meaning to *to think up* (we *think up* an idea, an excuse, etc.).

97. We continued to walk despite heavy snow starting to fall. (**EVEN**) → We kept on *walking even though it* started to snow heavily.

98. Almost all the tickets for the play on Broadway have been sold. (**HARDLY**) → There are *hardly any tickets left* for the play on Broadway.

99. Do you think it is likely that Rob will pass the exams he has signed up for? (**CHANCE**) → Do you think Rob *has/stands any chance of passing* the exams he has signed up for?

100. 'Do you know the cost of the tickets?' Henry asked me. (**MUCH**) → Henry asked me If I *knew how much the tickets* were.

101. We had to complete all the tasks before we could leave. (**COMPLETED**) → We couldn't *leave until we had completed* all the tasks.

102. We had not expected the conversations to be so animated. (**BETTER**) → The conversations *were better than we had* expected.

103. If Phil doesn't train harder, he'll never make the team. (**DOES**) → Phil will never make the team unless *he does (some)* more training.

104. She asked me, 'What do you think of the party?' (**LIKE**) → She asked me, 'How *did you like* the party?'

105. I signed up for the proficiency examination a month ago. (**SINCE**) → It *is/has been a month since* I signed up for the examination.

106. They say the notorious criminals fled to Mexico. (**HAVE**) → The notorious criminals *are said to have fled* to Mexico.

107. Because of the demonstrations, the police wouldn't let us park in the city centre. (**ALLOWED**) → We *were not allowed to park* in the city centre because of the demonstrations.

108. 'Did you see the new film released last weekend?' my boyfriend asked me. (**SEEN**) → My boyfriend wanted to *know if I had seen* the new film released last weekend.

109. Whatever you say, I won't believe you. (**MATTER**) → I won't believe you, no *matter what you* say.

110. Maybe the students have forgotten that the time of the meeting was changed. (**MIGHT**) → The students *might have forgotten* that the time of the meeting was changed.

111. My mother made me stay up late to cram for an examination. (**TO**) → I *was made to stay* up late by my mother to cram for an examination.

<u>Note(s)</u>: Someone "makes you *do* something", but you "are made *to* do something" (by someone). In the **passive voice**, we use the **infinitive** with *to*.

112. My grandparents were determined to pay for our holidays. (**INSISTED**) → My grandparents *insisted on paying* for our holidays.

113. I failed to persuade my students to sign up for the exams. (**SUCCEED**) → I *did not succeed in persuading* my students to sign up for the exams.

114. 'I would prefer you not to use your phone on the train,' the mother told her daughter. (**MIND**) → The mother told her daughter, 'Would *you mind not using* your phone on the train?'

115. 'Don't leave yet, will you?' she asked me. (**RATHER**) → I would *rather you did not leave* yet.

116. This student sometimes finds it difficult to stick to rules. (**TROUBLE**) → This student sometimes *has trouble (in) sticking* to rules.

117. 'Do you think Angela is likely to change her mind?' Jane asked. (**CHANCE**) → Jane asked, 'Is there *a/any chance of Angela changing* her mind?'

118. You ought to have filled up the tank before we left. (**CARELESS**) → It was *careless of you not to* have filled up the tank before we left.

119. Paula is the only student who has replied to the e-mail so far. (**NOBODY**) → Apart *from Paula, nobody* has replied to the e-mail so far.

120. More people live in urban areas nowadays than in the countryside. (**MANY**) → Nowadays, there are *not as many people living* in the countryside as in urban areas.

Note(s): The comparison ("as... as") can be better understood if we rewrite what is understood: "Nowadays, there are not as many people living in the countryside *as there are (people living)* in urban areas".

121. I have a suspicion that he is not a dependable colleague. (**SUSPECT**) → I *suspect him of not being* a dependable colleague.

Note(s): Here are some interesting (near-) synonym(s) of *dependable*: *staunch, steady, trustworthy*; opposite(s): *undependable, untrustworthy*. Related word(s): *dependability* (**noun**).

122. That's the hotel where we stayed last year. (**IN**) → That's the hotel *in which we stayed/which we stayed in* last year.

Note(s): The second option can be rephrased with *that*: "That's the hotel *that* we stayed in/at last year."

123. I don't like Pete because he's very mean. (**REASON**) → Pete's *meanness is the reason* why I don't like him.

124. I intended to leave earlier, but I decided to finish some reports instead. (**GOING**) → I *was going to leave* earlier, but I decided to finish some reports instead.

125. The father of that boy is a highly celebrated actor. (**WHOSE**) → That's *the boy whose father is* a highly celebrated actor.

126. I didn't have much money, but we were happy because we had each other. (**HAVING**) → In spite *of not having* much money, we were happy because we had each other.

Note(s): The answer can be rephrased as: "*Despite* not having..." (notice that *despite* is never followed by the **preposition** *of*). Both *in spite of* and *despite* can be followed by the **gerund**.

127. We enjoyed the camping trip, even though the weather was awful. (**SPITE**) → We enjoyed the camping trip, *in spite of the fact* that the weather was awful.

128. I don't like camping very much. I'd rather stay in a comfortable hotel. (**KEEN**) → I am *not very keen on* camping. I'd rather stay in a comfortable hotel.

Note(s): Some interesting collocations for *keen* include: *especially, particularly, really.* (Near-) synonym(s): *eager, enthusiastic*; opposite(s): *apathetic, uninterested.* Related word(s): *keenness* (**noun**), *keenly* (**adverb**).

129. M. de Assis was an extremely talented Brazilian writer. (**BRAZIL'S**) → M. de Assis was one of *Brazil's most talented* writers.

130. The Empire State building is not as tall as The World Trade Center. (**THAN**) → The World Trade Center building *is taller than* the Empire State.

131. It's a lot easier to learn a language by picking it up on the streets than from books alone. (**MUCH**) → You can learn a language *much more easily* when you pick it up on the streets than from books alone.

132. There's no point in arguing any further. (**POINTLESS**) → It *is pointless to argue* any further.

Note(s): The **gerund** is also possible after *pointless* ("It is pointless arguing..."), though less common.

133. It's impossible to put into words what I felt. (**NOT**) → What *I felt is not possible* to put into words.

134. If I accept this job, I'll have to commute into the city centre every day. (**MEAN**) → Accepting this job *will mean having to commute* into the city centre every day.

135. Sarah is regretful that she gave up school so easily. (**HAVING**) → Sarah *regrets having given up* school so easily.

Note(s): The **gerund** alone is enough to refer to the past: "Sarah regrets *giving up* school so easily."

136. Eric admitted that he had stolen the money. (**TO**) → Eric admitted *to having* stolen the money.

Note(s): As we have just pointed out above, this can also be rephrased by using the **gerund**, as in: "Eric admitted to *stealing...*".

137. 'How about going to the cinema?' she asked us. (**SHALL**) → She said, 'Let's *go to the cinema, shall* we?'

138. I've found some old pictures by chance in a drawer. (**ACROSS**) → I have *come/stumbled across* some old pictures in a drawer.

Note(s): A formal synonym of *to come across* is *to encounter*.

139. 'I'll drive if you feel like a rest, Dad,' his daughter said. (**OVER**) → The daughter offered to take *over if her dad felt* like a rest.

Note(s): As used in the answer, the **phrasal verb** *to take over* can be followed by an **object**: "If you're tired, I'll take over (*the driving*)."

140. They didn't once offer us a word of support. (**WERE**) → Not once *were we offered* a word of support.

Note(s): Note the **active** version of the answer: "Not once *did they offer us...*"

141. Whatever is the time? (**EARTH**) → What *on earth is* the time?

142. Both of the vending machines were out of order. (**OF**) → Neither *of the vending machines was* working.

Note(s): Informally, "neither of" takes a **plural verb**: "Neither of the vending machines *were* working."

143. Your nails need trimming. (**GET**) → You *need to get your nails* trimmed.

144. You will avoid many problems if you make your reservation in advance. (**ADVISABLE**) → It would *be advisable if you* made your reservation in advance.

<u>Note(s)</u>: 1) The **adjective** *advisable* can be followed by the **to-infinitive**: "It would be advisable *to make* your reservation...". 2) (Near-) synonyms of *advisable* include: *desirable*, *prudent*, *wise*, etc. Related word(s): *advisability* (**noun**), *advisably* (**adverb**).

145. I have never come across such a terrible book before. (**WORST**) → This is *the worst book I have* ever come across.

146. By next year, Jones will be celebrating thirty years in the field of English teaching. (**WORKING**) → By next year, Jones *will have been working* in the field of English teaching for thirty years.

147. The idea of dying can be frightening for many people. (**FRIGHTENED**) → A lot of people *are frightened by* the idea of dying.

<u>Note(s)</u>: Note that *to frighten* is a **verb** (from *fright* + **suffix** *-en*). It is also worth noting the related **phrasal verb** *to frighten sb/sth off*: "Be quiet, will you? Don't *frighten* the birds *off*!"

148. No fewer than five assistants are needed to help. (**LEAST**) → We *need at least five* assistants to help.

149. 'Can I borrow your book?' he asked. (**LEND**) → He asked me *if I could lend him* my book.

150. I cannot stop myself from crying when I read this author's novels. (**HELP**) → I cannot *help but* cry when I read this author's novels.

<u>Note(s)</u>: We can cross out *but* and use the **gerund**, with a similar meaning: "I can't help crying...".

ADVANCED (C1)

151. It is highly unlikely that I will pass the driving test. (**ODDS**) → The *odds are against me/my passing* the driving test.

152. Call on us any time you're around. (**HAPPEN**) → If you *(ever) happen to be* around, call on us.

153. If he worked harder, would you recommend him for promotion? (**WORK**) → Were *he to work* harder, would you recommend him for promotion?

Note(s): Also note that the answer can be reworded as: "If he were/was to work..." (*was* is colloquial).

154. I had just reached the car when it began to pour with rain. (**THAN**) → No sooner *had I reached the car than* it began to pour with rain.

Note(s): The structure beginning with "no sooner..." is usually followed by *than*, but *when* is also possible (less common).

155. I wanted to get a painter to redo my bedroom before I travelled, but I didn't have the time. (**HAD**) → I would like *to have had my bedroom redone* before I travelled, but I didn't have the time.

156. 'John wrote the song, not George,' Paul said. (**IT**) → According to Paul, *it was John who/that wrote* the song, not George.

157. I knew nothing at all about who the package belonged to. (**ABSOLUTELY**) → I had *absolutely no idea whose package* it was.

158. Even if it is expensive, they want to stay at the five-star hotel. (**MAY**) → Expensive *as/though it may be/seem*, they want to stay at the five-star hotel.

159. Unless someone is late, we should be able to cover all the points in today's lesson. (**TURNS**) → So long *as everybody turns up on* time, we should be able to cover all the points in today's lesson.

Note(s): 1) It is usually accepted that "so... as" is not just as frequent as its corresponding "as... as" (that is, "*As* long *as* everybody..."). 2) *To turn up* can be replaced with *to show up*: "So long as everybody *shows up*...".

160. If you don't tell truth, the camping trip will be cancelled. (**MEAN**) → Your failure to tell *the truth will/would mean cancelling* the camping trip.

161. My sister works much harder than I do. (**NOWHERE**) → I'm *nowhere near(ly) as hardworking as* my sister is.

162. It's the first time she has been here, so it is possible that she got lost. (**HAVE**) → She *may/might/could have got lost, since/as* it is the first time she has been here.

163. 'How long will it take for Mark to recover from his illness, Peter?' asked Jane. (**GET**) → Jane asked Peter how long he thought it *would take (for) Mark to get* over his illness.

164. Joe regretted speaking so bluntly to his teacher. (**MORE**) → Joe wished *he had spoken more* tactfully to his teacher.

165. You really have to make a decision about your future. (**MIND**) → It's high *time you made up your mind* about your future.

166. 'Complete your assignments first, and then you can hang out with your friends,' my father said. (**LONG**) → My father agreed to let me hang out with my friends *as/so long as I completed* my assignments first.

167. People think the terrorists have fled from the country. (**THOUGHT**) → The terrorists *are thought to have fled* from the country.

Note(s): The **preposition** *from* can be crossed out: "... are thought to have fled the country".

168. Henry thought of organizing a house-warming party for the new neighbours. (**CAME**) → Henry *came up with the idea of* organizing a house-warming party for the new neighbours.

169. Thanks to the scholarship, I got into university. (**FOR**) → If it *had not been for* the scholarship, I wouldn't have got into university.

Note(s): For emphasis, we can use inversion and drop out *if*: "Had it not been for the scholarship, I wouldn't have got into university".

170. They're decorating my room, so it is in an awful mess. (**DONE**) → I am *having my room done up*, so it is in an awful mess.

171. When his car broke down, Michael phoned a mechanic. (**DID**) → When his car broke down, what *Michael did was (to) phone* a mechanic.

172. It has been reported that there are massive landslides blocking the motorway. (**REPORTS**) → There *have been reports of* massive landslides blocking the motorway.

173. It seems that his participation in the scheme is not evident at all. (**APPEARS**) → There *appears to be no evidence* whatsoever that he participated in the scheme.

174. It seems that there is no evidence to support the accusations made against him. (**SEEM**) → There *does not seem to be any* evidence to support the accusations made against him.

175. There are a few aspects of my job that I don't like, but by and large I enjoy it. (**WHOLE**) → Though there are a few aspects of my job that I don't like, *on the whole* I enjoy it.

176. It's useless to try to make him change his mind, as he is very stubborn. (**USE**) → There *is no use (in) trying* to make him change his mind, as he is very stubborn.

177. My parents allow me to do almost everything, but they don't let me drink or smoke. (**LINE**) → My parents allow me to do almost everything, but they *draw the line at drinking* or smoking.

178. I absolutely hate it when my teachers talk down to me, as if I were an idiot. (**BEING**) → I strongly object *to being talked down to by* my teachers, as if I were an idiot.

179. She will just avert her gaze whenever her father tells her off for her unseemly behaviour. (**AWAY**) → She will just *look away from* her father whenever he tells her off for her unseemly behaviour.

Note(s): Some (near-) synonyms of *unseemly* include: *improper, inappropriate, untoward, unbecoming,* etc. Opposite(s): *seemly*. Related word(s): *unseemliness* (noun).

180. If he keeps neglecting his professional duties like that, he'll lose his job. (**FIRED**) → He'll *be/get fired from* his job if he keeps neglecting his professional duties like that.

181. The children weren't listening to their parents, but they didn't mind. (**ATTENTION**) → The children weren't *paying attention to what their parents* were saying, but they didn't mind.

182. Given that Ann has no experience, will she be able to carry out such an ambitious project? (**AFFECT**) → Will Ann's *inexperience/lack of experience affect her ability* to carry out such an ambitious project?

183. 'We won't make any changes to the project for the time being,' my boss said. (**WHATSOEVER**) → My boss said no *changes whatsoever would be made* to the project for the time being.

184. 'Don't forget to keep in touch,' said my friend as he got in the car and drove off. (**NOT**) → My friend reminded *me not to forget to stay* in touch as he got in the car and drove off.

185. He no longer thinks he can get a pass grade until the end of the semester. (**HOPE**) → He's given **up (all/any) hope of getting** a pass grade until the end of the semester.

186. 'Send my regards to your parents, won't you?' my friend asked me. (**REMEMBER**) → My friend asked me, '**Remember me to** your parents, won't you?'

Note(s): The **tag question** *"won't you?"* may also be *"will you?"* with the **imperative**. *"Would you?"* is also possible and conveys more politeness: *"... remember me to your parents, will/would you?"*

187. I don't think the family business will make substantial profits this year, considering the economic situation. (**SURPRISED**) → Considering the economic situation, I **would be surprised if** the family business made any profits this year.

188. We have no intention of making changes to the academic programme. (**AHEAD**) → The academic programme will **go ahead (exactly) according** to plan.

189. I don't know what I would've done in the same situation as you. (**BEEN**) → Had **I been in** the same situation as you, I don't know what I would've done.

190. I was just about to leave when the telephone rang. (**POINT**) → I was **on the point of leaving** when the telephone rang.

191. Her boss told her that no one should be allowed to interrupt the meeting. (**CIRCUMSTANCES**) → 'Under **no circumstances is the meeting** to be interrupted,' her boss told her.

192. Although the players train really hard, they never make it to the finals. (**MATTER**) → They never make it to the finals, **no matter how hard** the players train.

193. Despite her best efforts, she never seems to get good grades. (HOWEVER) → She never seems to get good grades, *however hard she* tries.

194. The teachers rarely seem to consider the needs of the students. (ACCOUNT) → The students' needs rarely *seem to be taken into account* by the teachers.

195. Sarah's father said it was her own fault the party was ruined. (PUT) → Sarah's father *put the blame on her for* the party being ruined.

196. I'm sorry I said that you looked ugly in your new dress. (BACK) → I *take back what I said about* you looking ugly in your new dress.

197. There were far too many people at the party, but I still had a great time. (MAY) → There *may have been far too many* people at the party, but I still had a great time.

198. 'You've left my mobile phone on the bus, Jane!' Sandra shouted. (ACCUSED) → Jane *was accused of leaving/having left Sandra's* mobile phone on the bus.

199. Although he didn't have any experience, Robert was offered the position. (SPITE) → Robert was offered the position, *in spite of his* complete inexperience.

200. There were far too many applicants for the position, but we chose only a few to be interviewed. (SHORTLISTED) → There were far too many applicants for the position, but only a few *were shortlisted for the* interview.

Note(s): When you *narrow down* something (such as a list), you make it shorter: "The list of books competing for the prize *was narrowed down* from ten to five titles".

201. I don't usually judge the way people speak, but I couldn't help noticing his pronounced accent. (HABIT) → I'm not *in the habit of*

judging people's manner of speaking, but I couldn't help noticing his pronounced accent.

202. There were many wonderful compositions, but only three received special praise. (**SINGLED**) → There were many wonderful compositions, but only three *were singled out for* special praise.

203. He should have learned to fend for himself by now. (**HIGH**) → It's *high time he learned* to fend for himself.

204. I'm not really sure, but I'd say it'll be very expensive. (**HEAD**) → Off the *top of my head*, I'd say it'll be very expensive.

205. He's studying hard in order to obtain a scholarship at college. (**VIEW**) → He's studying hard *with a view to obtaining* a scholarship at college.

Note(s): Also *with an eye to*: "... studying hard *with an eye to* obtaining...".

206. If Richard withdraws from the race, Peter might come out victorious. (**STANDS**) → If Richard withdraws from the race, Peter *stands a chance of coming* out victorious.

Note(s): Useful collocations with *chance* include: *remote*, *slight*, *slim/fair*, *real*, *strong* (**adjectives**). Note that *fat chance* is slang and currently means *no chance at all*: 'Do you think he'll turn up at the party?' 'Fat chance (of that)!'

207. I'm completely sure your parents are already in the know about everything by now. (**BOUND**) → Your parents *are bound to have found* out about everything by now.

208. If you want this job, you must be able to think and make decisions quickly. (**FEET**) → The *ability to think on your feet* is essential if you want this job.

Note(s): If you can *think on your feet*, you're also able to *act on the spur (of the moment)*, that is to say, by improvising, without previous thought or planning.

209. It appears that the financial climate will start to look up very soon. (**INDICATION**) → There is _every indication to suggest_ that the financial climate will start to look up very soon.

Note(s): The **phrasal verb** to look up can also be used to talk about the weather: "At long last, the weather is starting to look up again". With the same meaning, we can also say: brighten (up), improve, etc. (collocation patterns). 2) We may drop out to suggest ("There is every indication ~~to suggest~~ that..."), but at CAE you must use at least three words.

210. I feel better now that I have opened up about my feelings. (**CHEST**) → Now that I _have got it off my chest_, I feel better.

211. The event will very likely be called off. (**LIKELYHOOD**) → There _is every likelihood of the event_ being called off.

Note(s): 1) The **noun** likelihood can be followed by a **that-clause**: "There is every likelihood that the event will be called off". 2) Every is followed by a **noun** to show emphasis.

212. It is certain that people will protest against the demolition of that historic building. (**BOUND**) → There are _bound to be protests_ against the demolition of that historic building.

213. My daughter was almost crying when I broke the bad news to her. (**VERGE**) → My daughter was _on the verge of breaking_ down in tears when I broke the bad news to her.

214. I only read that book because it was recommended to me. (**IF**) → I would _never have read that book if_ it hadn't been recommended to me.

215. It seems as though we completely misunderstood what the purpose of our mission was. (**HAVE**) → There seems _to have been a complete misunderstanding_ about the purpose of our mission.

Note(s): The **noun** misunderstanding collocates with the following **adjectives** (close in meaning): _fundamental, gross, profound, serious, terrible._ If it is not very serious, you can say 'a _slight_ misunderstanding'.

216. There are rumours that the corrupt politician involved in the scandals has already submitted his resignation. (**RUMOURED**) → The corrupt politician *is rumoured to have handed* in his resignation already.

217. If you hadn't helped me, I wouldn't have been able to complete the task. (**OTHERWISHE**) → Thank you for your help, *otherwise I wouldn't have completed* the task.

218. If you insist on going to sleep late, naturally you'll feel tired all day. (**GO**) → If *you will go to sleep* late, naturally you'll feel tired all day.

Note(s): We do not normally use *will* in the **if-clause**, but we use it when criticism is implied. Without it, the clause would mean basically the same.

219. A true story provides the basis for the film about that singer. (**BASED**) → The film about that singer *is based on* a true story.

220. If Julia hadn't supported and encouraged us, they would've turned down our project. (**SUPPORT**) → But *for Julia's support and encouragement*, they would've turned down our project.

Note(s): The **phrasal verb** *to turn down* is separable: "... they would've turned our project down". It usually collocates with *application, offer, proposal*, etc. (Near-) synonym(s): *to reject*.

221. She always confides in her best friend. (**TRUSTS**) → She always *trusts her best friend with her* secrets.

222. A recent study found that there's a link between stress and heart disease. (**BORNE**) → The link between stress and heart disease *is borne out by the* findings of a recent study.

223. I am not strong enough to lift this heavy box. (**STRONGER**) → If I *were stronger, I would be able* to lift this heavy box.

224. Don't you think you'd benefit from a few days off? (**DO**) → Don't you think a *few days off would do you* a lot of good?

225. We have given school supplies to the poorer students. (**PROVIDED**) → The poorer students *have been provided with* school supplies.

226. Can you explain how the money disappeared? (**ACCOUNT**) → How *do you account for the disappearance* of the money?

227. Rick is in the seventh grade now because he didn't pass his finals last year. (**WOULD**) → Rick *would be in the eighth grade* now if he had passed his finals last year.

228. People generally believe the old church dates from the tenth century. (**WIDELY**) → The old church *is widely believed to date* from the tenth century.

229. He succeeded in talking his classmates into taking part in his project. (**MANAGED**) → He *managed to talk* his classmates into taking part in his project.

230. She is not as mean as people believe she is. (**MADE**) → She's not as mean as she *is made out to* be.

231. They resolved to bring the issue up at the next meeting. (**WOULD**) → It *was resolved that the issue would* be brought up at the next meeting.

232. 'I haven't smoked for a long time,' he told me. (**STOPPED**) → He told me that he *had stopped smoking (a) long (time)* ago.

233. She's proud of the fact that she's always early for appointments. (**PRIDES**) → She *prides herself on never being* late for appointments.

234. Please hold on a moment, and I'll get back to you right away. (**WILL**) → If *you will hold on* a moment, I'll get back to you right away.
Note(s): We do not normally use *will* in the **if-clause**, but we use it to convey willingness or to sound more polite.

235. Who do you think accounts for the failure of the project? (**HELD**) → Who do you think is *to be held accountable for* the project going wrong?

Note(s): Useful (near-) synonyms of *accountable* include: *answerable, culpable, liable,* etc. Opposite(s): *unaccountable.* Related word(s): *accountability* (**noun**), *accountably* (**adverb**).

236. 'You can't use the office computers for anything except work', my boss said. (**MEANT**) → My boss said we were *not meant to use/make use of* the office computers for anything except work.

237. Apart from Michael, no other teachers were selected for the course overseas. (**BE**) → Michael *was the only teacher to be* selected for the course overseas.

238. He enjoyed the film, but he wondered whether the events depicted were historically accurate. (**ACCURATELY**) → Although he enjoyed the film, he wasn't sure *about how accurately depicted the events* were.

239. If you hadn't given me a helping hand, I wouldn't have got all the work done. (**GIVING**) → But *for you/your giving* me a helping hand, I wouldn't have got all the work done.

240. No matter how hard he studied, he never succeeded in getting an honour pass. (**THOUGH**) → Hard *though he studied*, he never succeeded in getting an honour pass.

Note(s): Or: "Hard *as* he studied...".

241. The teacher gave me his word that he would allow me to resit the exam. (**ASSURED**) → The teacher *assured me that I would be* allowed to resit the exam.

242. The employee never really thought that he would end up being promoted. (**CROSSED**) → It never *crossed the employee's* mind that he would end up being promoted.

243. The students were impressed by their teacher's ability to remember all of their names. (**ABLE**) → The students found it *impressive that their teacher was able* to remember all of their names.

244. The notorious criminal disappeared with absolutely no indication of his whereabouts. (**TRACE**) → The notorious criminal disappeared, *leaving no trace whatsoever/whatever of his/her* whereabouts.

245. 'I'm sure the other witnesses' testimony will lend support to mine,' the defendant said. (**BEAR**) → The defendant said that the other witnesses' testimony *would bear out what he had* said.

246. Whatever time she leaves home, Lucy never seems to be able to get to school on time. (**MATTER**) → No *matter what time/how early she sets* off from home, Lucy never seems to be able to get to school on time.

247. It is Chris's responsibility to ensure that all the equipment is working properly before the concerts. (**CHARGE**) → Chris's *in charge of making sure* that all the equipment is working properly before the concerts.

248. George was going to throw a house-warming party to welcome the new neighbours, but apparently he's decided against it. (**MIND**) → It appears *(that) George has changed his mind* about throwing a party to welcome the new neighbours.

249. You're re forever changing your mind, John! I can't understand you. (**FIGURE**) → You're forever changing your mind; that's why I can't *figure you out*, John.

250. He was looking forward to visiting Paris again. (**HARDLY**) → He *could hardly wait to visit* Paris again.

251. You must have confused me with someone else. (**MISTAKEN**) → I think *you must have mistaken me for* someone else.

252. Paul prides himself on always being on time for work. (**PRIDE**) → Paul takes *pride in never being* late for work.

253. What is the exact difference between advanced and proficiency certificates? (**DIFFER**) → How *exactly do certificates differ from advanced* to proficiency?

254. In the end, it's all a matter of power and status. (**DOWN**) → In the end, it _**all comes/boils down to**_ power and status.

255. How on earth did she deceive you with her story? (**TAKEN**) → However could _**you have been taken in by**_ her story?

256. They blamed the accident on a cursory inspection of the vehicle. (**SAID**) → A cursory inspection of the vehicle was _**said to be the cause of**_ the accident.

Note(s): Some interesting (near-) synonyms of _cursory_ include: _hasty, perfunctory, slapdash,_ etc. Opposite(s): _meticulous, painstaking, thorough._ Related word(s): _cursoriness_ (**noun**), _cursorily_ (**adverb**).

257. The total came to just over five thousand pounds. (**WORKED**) → The total _**worked out at**_ just over five thousand pounds.

258. I still haven't fully understood how I succeeded in passing the exam. (**SUNK**) → It _**hasn't sunk in yet**_ how I managed to pass the exam.

Note(s): 1) _Yet_ may go after the **auxiliary** _have_ ("It hasn't _yet_ sunk in..."); this is less common, though. 2) _To sink in_ (of ideas, words, etc.) can be used **intransitively**: "It took me some time for the bad news to _sink in_" (that is, "for me to fully understand/grasp").

259. We eventually had to take a taxi to the airport. (**ENDED**) → We _**ended up having to take**_ a taxi to the airport.

Note(s): 1) Note this (near-) synonym of _to end up_: _to wind up_ ("We _wound up_ taking a taxi..."). 2) Note this informal, related **adjective**: "Don't get all _wound up_ by what he's saying. Just ignore him" (that is, _annoyed, upset_).

260. He was given the axe because he was involved in an embezzling scheme. (**ACCOUNT**) → He was given the axe _**on account of his**_ involvement in an embezzling scheme.

261. I'll be speaking as a representative of the company which I work for. (**BEHALF**) → I'll be speaking _**on behalf of the company**_ which I work for.

262. He called pretending that he needed to borrow some books, but I knew he was lying. (**PRETENCE**) → He called *on/under the pretence of needing* to borrow some books, but I knew he was lying.

Note(s): In *AmE*, *pretense*, with an *s*. One of its (near-) synonyms is the **true cognate** *pretext*: "He called her on the *pretext* of needing..." Other (near-) synonyms include: *deceit, excuse, guise,* etc. Opposite(s): *sincerity*. Related word(s): *pretend* (**verb**), *pretentiousness* (**noun**), *pretentiously* (**adverb**).

263. Joel was the ideal candidate, so not surprisingly he was awarded the scholarship. (**CAME**) → Joel was the ideal candidate, so it *came as no surprise that* he was awarded the scholarship.

264. There has been a drop in the price of petrol over the last few months. (**COME**) → The price of petrol *has come down* over the last few months.

265. 'Surely the sun will be scorching hot later, so why don't you apply some sunscreen?' she warned me. (**BETTER**) → She warned me, 'You *had better put* some sunscreen on. Surely the sun will be scorching hot later.'

Note(s): Some interesting (near-) synonyms of *scorching* include: *blistering, fiery, sizzling, sweltering,* etc. Opposite(s): *cool*. Related word(s): *scorchingly* (**adverb**).

266. 'You should stop your students using their mobile phones during the classes,' Mary's colleague told her. (**LET**) → Mary's colleague advised her *not to let the students use* their mobile phones during the classes.

Note(s): *To let* is followed by **object** (*the students*) + **infinitive** without *to* (*use*); *to allow* is followed by **object** and **infinitive** with *to*: "... advised her not to allow *the students to use*...".

267. Harry missed his train because we was late leaving for the station. (**LEFT**) → If only *Harry had left in/on time* for the station, he wouldn't have missed his train.

Note(s): *In time* means with enough time, while *on time* means *punctually*.

268. The guidelines for students' conduct in class need to be thoroughly revised. (**THOROUGH**) → There *needs to be a thorough revision* to the guidelines for students' conduct in class.

269. The unemployment rate dropped gradually as the economy began to improve. (**GRADUAL**) → There *was a gradual drop in* the unemployment rate as the economy began to improve.

270. The changes to the exam format didn't make any difference to the candidates. (**CONSEQUENCE**) → The changes to the exam format weren't *of any consequence* to the candidates.

Note(s): Note the **adjective** *inconsequential*, which is close in meaning to *unimportant*; (near-) synonyms include: *negligible*, *minor*. Opposite(s): *significant*. Related word(s): *inconsequentially* (**adverb**).

271. His colleagues regarded him so highly that he had everyone's support. (**HELD**) → He was *held in such high regard* by his colleagues that he had everyone's support.

272. We owe our clients some compensation, as we apparently gave them incorrect information. (**APPEAR**) → We owe our clients some compensation, as they *appear to have been* given incorrect information.

273. If he passes his entrance exams, which is unlikely, he'll study at one of the Ivy League universities. (**EVENT**) → In the *unlikely event that he passes/will pass* his entrance exams, he'll study at one of the Ivy League universities.

274. Please make sure all our customers are satisfied with the hotel's service. (**SEE**) → Please *see to it that* all our customers are satisfied with the hotel's service.

275. The director insisted that it might be a good idea if he participated in an intensive training programme. (**TAKE**) → The director insisted *that he (should) take part* in an intensive training program.

Note(s): The formal **subjunctive** (more commonly found in *AmE*) does not require an "s" for the third person ("... insisted that he *take*"); in *BrE*, it is more usual to use *should* instead ("... insisted that he *should* take..."), but the exam accepts both answers.

276. This film has a very strong chance of being nominated for the prize. (**HIGHLY**) → It is <u>highly likely that this film will</u> be nominated for the prize.

277. 'You really must spend the weekend with us,' she told us. (**SPENDING**) → She insisted <u>on us/our spending</u> the weekend with them.

278. If my sister hadn't told my father about the prang, he wouldn't have argued with me. (**FOR**) → Had it <u>not been for my sister telling</u> my father about the prang, he wouldn't have argued with me.

Note(s): A *prang* is a *fender bender*, that is to say, an accident in which the vehicles involved are only slightly damaged. The latter is more common in *AmE*.

279. We were never aware at any moment that we were breaking the law. (**TIME**) → At <u>no time were we (ever)</u> aware that we were breaking the law.

280. The students are on very good terms with their teachers. (**GET**) → The students <u>get on (very) well</u> with their teachers.

281. They believe Sarah failed her driving test because she was very nervous. (**DOWN**) → Sarah's failure in her driving test <u>was put down to (her)</u> nervousness.

282. 'Why didn't I ask him out? He might have accepted!' thought Jane. (**ASKED**) → 'If <u>only I had asked</u> him out, he might have accepted!' thought Jane.

283. Even though he had been severely injured in the accident, he recovered completely. (**PULL**) → He managed <u>to pull through</u>, even though he had been severely injured in the accident.

284. 'I absolutely hate what the critics are writing about my songs,' Billy said. (**OBJECTED**) → Billy _strongly objected to what was being_ written about his songs by the critics.

285. When he started his course, he soon realised that he had made the wrong choice. (**LONG**) → It did not _take long for him to realise_ he had made the wrong choice when he started his course.

Note(s): The answer may be rephrased as: "It did not take him long to realise…".

286. We could always rely on Joel to confront our teacher if she became too authoritarian. (**STAND**) → Joel could always be _relied on to stand up to_ our teacher if she became too authoritarian.

Note(s): Useful (near-) synonym(s) of _authoritarian_ include: _despotic, dictatorial, intransigent, uncompromising, unyielding_; opposite(s): _flexible_. Do not confuse this word with _authoritative_ (= dependable, trustworthy).

287. We can't just pretend that everything will turn out all right in the end. (**DECEIVE**) → We can't just _deceive ourselves into thinking/believing_ that everything will turn out all right in the end.

288. I don't understand! You can't have watched the same film as I have. (**BEEN**) → I don't understand! It _can't have been_ the same film that you watched.

289. I had no interest whatsoever in the offer. (**LEAST**) → I wasn't _the least (bit) interested_ in the offer.

Note(s): You can also say "I wasn't interested _in the slightest_", with a close meaning.

290. It is not certain that the tournament will take place. (**MEANS**) → It is _by no means certain whether or_ not the tournament will take place.

291. I tried many times; it was useless to warn him, though. (**TRIED**) → I tried _and tried, but_ it was useless to warn him.

Note(s): The answer can be rephrased as: "I tried *over and over* again..." or 'I tried *time and (time) again*".

292. I absolutely hate summer colds. In winter, they seem less nasty. (STAND) → What <u>I can't stand is</u> summer colds. In winter, they seem less nasty.

293. Their house was the last house one would expect to be broken into. (VERY) → Theirs <u>was the very last house</u> one would expect to be broken into.

294. One month passed before they published the results. (UNTIL) → Not <u>until one month had passed did</u> they publish the results.

295. I know you're under a lot of pressure, but don't vent your anger on me. (OUT) → I know you're under a lot of pressure, but I wish you <u>would not take it out on</u> me.

Note(s): Also note the expression *give vent to* (that is, *to express*).

296. I apologise in advance, but I have to touch on this thorny issue. (BRING) → I apologise in advance, but I <u>have to/must bring up</u> this thorny issue.

Note(s): *Thorny* useful (near-) synonym(s), in this context, include: *bothersome, delicate, unpleasant*, etc. (figurative, metaphorical meaning from *thorn*).

297. The writer has received a lot of criticism from the more discerning readers. (COME) → The writer <u>has come in for</u> a lot of criticism from the more discerning readers.

Note(s): Useful (near-) synonyms of *discerning* include: *judicious, knowledgeable, shrewd*. Opposite(s): *stupid, undiscerning*. Related word(s): *discernment* (**noun**), *discerningly* (**adverb**).

298. You need to save some money that you can use as a last resort. (FALL) → You need to save some money to <u>fall back on</u> as a last resort.

Note(s): In the phrase *as a last resort*, the word *resort* (**noun**) has these useful (near-) synonyms: *expedient* and *resource*.

299. In the end, the students managed to avoid being punished harshly. (**LIGHT**) → The students got *off/away with (just) a light* punishment in the end.

Note(s): 1) We can use the corresponding **adverb** *lightly*: "The students *got off lightly* in the end" (or, informally, *easy*: "They got off *easy*") (not *easily*). 2) Here are some useful collocations for *punishment*: *draconian, harsh, severe, fitting* (**adjectives**); *administer, deserve, inflict, take* (**verbs**). Note that '*strict* punishment' is not a very common pattern.

300. I'm pressed for time at work to meet tight deadlines. (**CLOCK**) → I *am working against/around the clock* to meet tight deadlines at work.

Note(s): It might be worth taking a look at these collocations with *deadline*: (a) *strict* deadline(s) (**adjective**); *to meet, to miss* (a) deadline(s) (**verbs**).

301. He sometimes found it difficult to make himself understood. (**MEANING**) → Sometimes he had *difficulty/trouble (in) getting his meaning* across.

302. I wish I could give my boss a piece of my mind and then hand in my notice. (**MIND**) → I have *half a mind* to give my boss a piece of my mind and then hand in my notice.

Note(s): 1) The answer may be reworded as "I have a *good* mind to give...". 2) A *notice* is a *resignation letter*. Also note the expression *to be in/of two minds*, that is to say, to be indecisive.

303. Havoc followed directly as a consequence of the tornadoes that swept across the country. (**WAKE**) → Havoc followed *in the wake of* the tornadoes that swept across the country.

Note(s): Useful (near-) synonyms of *havoc* include: *calamity, catastrophe, devastation, mayhem*. Phrase(s): to *play/wreak* havoc..., etc. Some useful collocations with *havoc* include: *cause, create* (**verbs**).

304. Curfew has been declared by the authorities because of the recent terrorist threats. (**OWING**) → Authorities have *declared curfew owing to* the recent terrorist threats.

305. The newspaper reviewers are levelling heavy criticism at the writer's new book. (**COMING**) → The newspaper reviewers are *coming down heavily on the writer's* new book.

Note(s): The **phrasal verb** *to come down on* generally means *to punish*, as in "The police is/are planning to *come/crack down on* drug dealing...".

306. Old-fashioned as their ideas may sound, they are valid to this day. (**HOLD**) → Their ideas may seem old-fashioned, but they *still hold good/true* to this day.

Note(s): Or, figuratively: "... hold *water* to this day".

307. Susan and her mother stopped being friends because of a pointless argument and haven't spoken to each other ever since. (**FALLEN**) → Susan and her mother *have fallen out over* a pointless argument and haven't spoken to each other ever since.

Note(s): There is an important distinction between *argument* and *discussion*. The latter is an exchange of ideas, a debate. If you mean *to quarrel*, you say *argument* or *an angry discussion*. Some useful collocation patterns (**adjectives**) for *argument* include: *bitter, fierce, heated, silly*, etc. Also note that *an argumentative person* is *confrontational, contentious, fractious, quarrelsome*, etc.

308. We wanted to continue our tour of the city centre but the weather didn't permit it. (**LIKE**) → We *would like to have carried/gone* on with our tour of the city centre but the weather didn't permit it.

309. This mystery is still waiting for an explanation. (**REMAINS**) → There *remains this mystery* still waiting for an explanation.

Note(s): *There* is being used here as an **empty subject**. *To remain* agrees in number with *this mystery*. In the plural, the "-s" is left out: "There *remain* these mysteries...". Also note the structure *there exist(s)*. "Many mysteries still exist in this world" becomes, with existential *there*, "There still exist many mysteries in this world".

310. It would be difficult for Laura to pay for all her expenses without the help of her friends. (**ENDS**) → Laura would have a lot of *difficulty (in) making ends meet if* it weren't for the help of her friends.

Note(s): The expression *to make (both) ends meet* reminds us of another expression, *hand-to-mouth*, as in "a *hand-to-mouth* existence", that is to say, with hardly enough money to live on.

311. I was most surprised to run into Adam at the party. (**VERY**) → Adam was *the very last person* I'd expect to meet at the party.

Note(s): Interesting (near-) synonym(s) of the **phrasal verb** *to run into* include: *to bump into, to encounter* (formal), *to run across, to stumble upon,* etc.

312. It surprised me to learn that John stopped smoking because he wanted to improve his health. (**SURPRISE**) → Much *to my surprise John gave up* smoking because he wanted to improve his health.

313. My adviser says she's been too busy to start marking my paper but promised she would do it as soon as possible. (**DOWN**) → My adviser says she *has not got down to marking* my paper yet but promised she would do that as soon as possible.

314. As a young adult, he still behaves like he used to in his teenage years. (**MUCH**) → As a young adult, he still behaves *in much the same way* as he did in his teenage years.

Note(s): Note that *like* (in the lead-in) is informal; *as* would be more adequate, as in the answer ("... in much the same way *as* he did...").

315. Sandra's offensive remarks make her mother angry, which is perfectly understandable. (**BLAME**) → Sandra's *mother is not to blame for* getting angry at her daughter's offensive remarks.

Note(s): 1) *To be not to blame* is a fixed pattern in which the **infinitive** (*to blame*), though **active** in form, has a **passive** sense in informal contexts. "She is not to *be* blam*ed*..." is standard grammar. 2) You can be angry *with/at* someone or something.

316. My boss only ever criticized my work and never really appreciated me. (**FAULT**) → My boss was forever *finding fault with* my work and never really appreciated me.

317. I've had the intention of replying to your email, but I haven't yet had any time to do so. (**MEANING**) → Though I *have been meaning to do so*, I haven't yet had any time to reply to your email.

Note(s): Although the position of *yet* is usually at the end of the sentence, in formal register it can come between the **auxiliary** and the **main verb** ("... haven't *yet* had..."). Also note that the lead-in can be rephrased as "... I *still* haven't had any time...".

318. My old car is not working well. It just won't start. (**PLAYING**) → My old car *is playing me* up. It just won't start.

Note(s): 1) You may leave out the **pronoun**: "The car is *playing up*..." if it is not necessary in the context. 2) Another interesting sense of *to play up* is *to behave badly*: "The children have been playing up all day".

319. I'm not really sure, but I think they've broken up. (**KNOWLEDGE**) → To *the best of my knowledge*, they've broken up.

Note(s): 1) This can be rephrased as: "As/So far as I know, they've broken up." 2) Notice that we use *to my knowledge* when we are certain about something ("To my knowledge, they've broken up" means "I know for certain/a fact (that) they've broken up").

320. I moved to France because I was deeply fascinated by this country. (**MUCH**) → I was deeply fascinated by France, so *much so that* I moved to this country.

Note(s): As an additional exercise, try rewriting the answer, beginning with *such*. Here's the key: "*Such was my fascination with France that I moved...*".

321. If you take your medicine as the doctor prescribed, you will recover very quickly. (**TIME**) → If you take your medicine as the doctor prescribed, you will recover in *no time at* all.

Note(s): Also, *in no time* (without the empathic *at all*), or *in next to no time*.

322. All the prisoners have to answer for their actions in case of misbehaviour. (**ANSWERABLE**) → All the prisoners must *be made answerable* for their actions in case of misbehavior.

Note(s): The answer may be rephrased with a close meaning as "... must be held *accountable* for misbehaviour". (Near-) synonyms of *answerable* include: *chargeable, liable, responsible*. Opposite(s): *unaccountable*. Related word(s): *answerability* (**noun**).

323. In next to no time, I'm sure you'll take to your new co-workers. (**LIKING**) → In next to no time, I'm sure you'll *develop/take a liking for* your new co-workers.

Note(s): When you *take to* someone, you like, or are on good terms with them; when you *take to* something, you get into a new habit: "When he retired, he took to drinking binges".

324. My brother was rude to me but I got my revenge on him. (**BACK**) → I paid *my brother back for him/his being* rude to me.

325. We definitely can't get this done in time. (**WAY**) → There is *no way we will be able* to get this done in time.

C2 – PROFICIENCY

326. She was determined to pass the final examinations. (**SET**) → She was dead *set on passing* the final examinations.

327. As soon as I got into the bathtub, I heard someone knocking on the door. (**SOONER**) → No *sooner did I get into the bathtub than* I heard someone knocking on the door.

<u>Note(s)</u>: *When* (instead of *than*) is also possible, though less common: "... into the bathtub *when* I...".

328. I was not sure if I wanted to stay. (**MINDS**) → I *was in/of two minds whether or not* to stay.

329. It took me a lot of time to find out what my condition was. (**DID**) → Only after a lot of time *did I find out* what my condition was.

330. Her first flight experience was a nightmare, but this didn't harm her at all. (**WORSE**) → Her first flight was a nightmare, but she *was none the worse for* this experience.

331. They say a visual presentation is more efficient than words. (**PAINTS**) → As the saying goes, 'A *picture paints a thousand* words'.

<u>Note(s)</u>: Or, more commonly: "A picture *is worth* a thousand words".

332. He was offended that his teacher called him a nuisance. (**OFFENCE**) → He took *offence at being called a nuisance by* his teacher.

333. She was slowly accepting the death of her cat. (**TERMS**) → She was slowly *coming to terms with the fact that* her cat had died.

334. He was offended by his teacher's accusations that he had cheated in the exam. (**EXCEPTION**) → He *took exception at/to being/having been accused* of cheating in the exam.

335. 'I would prefer to stay in, if you don't mind,' he told her. (**SOON**) → 'I would *just as soon* stay in, if you don't mind,' he told her.

336. Thank goodness you didn't come to the party. It was awful. (**WELL**) → It *is/was just as well (that)* you didn't come to the party. It was awful.

337. He mistakenly believes his mother will always be at his beck and call. (**GRANTED**) → He *takes it for granted that* his mother will always be at his beck and call.

Note(s): These verbs are (near-) synonyms of the expression *to take for granted*: *to assume, to presume, to suppose, to surmise*.

338. I have read the instructions carefully, but I haven't understood them at all. (**NONE**) → I have read the instructions carefully, but I'm *still none the* wiser.

Note(s): The answer can be rephrased as: "but still I'm not *any* the wiser".

339. Ann just couldn't imagine what she was in for. (**DID**) → Little *did Ann imagine* what she was in for.

Note(s): If you *are in for* something, you can expect something bad or unpleasant to happen: "Ann *is in for* a lot of criticism because of her decision"; 'It looks as though we'*re in for* a thunderstorm,' said the camp counselor.

340. 'Would you like to go away at the weekend?' he asked me. (**MOOD**) → He asked me *if/whether I was in the mood for going* away at the weekend.

341. Peter was exhausted and also had a nasty cold. (**ONLY**) → Not *only was Peter exhausted but (he) also* had a nasty cold.

Note(s): These are interesting (near-) synonyms of *nasty*: *awful, loathsome, noxious, obnoxious*. Apart from *nasty*, these adjectives also commonly collocate with *cold*: (suffer from) a *bad*, a *heavy*, a *slight* cold.

342. Do you mind if I watch TV while you're reading? (**OBJECTION**) → Do you *have any objection to my watching* TV while you're reading?

Note(s): From *objection* we can form the **adjective** *objectionable*, whose (near-) synonyms include: *abhorrent, deplorable, offensive, unacceptable*, etc.

343. His cold heart was completely devoid of feelings. (**WHATSOEVER**) → There were *no feelings whatsoever/whatever* in his cold heart.

344. It is difficult to predict how long it will take for him to recover. (**TELLING**) → There *is no telling how long his recovery will* take.

345. For me, her skill as an actress was most impressive. (**HOW**) → I was *most impressed by/with/at how skillful an actress she* was.

346. Everybody expected the politician to resign, so no one was surprised. (**CAME**) → The politician's *resignation came as no surprise to* anyone.

Note(s): In the exercise, *resignation* means *to step down* from power, *to abdicate* from it. Also notice this different meaning of *resignation*, whose (near-) synonyms include: *acceptance, forbearance, longanimity, passiveness*, etc. Opposite(s): *nonconformity*.

347. Everyone was surprised that the politician had resigned. (**SURPRISE**) → The politician had resigned, which *came as a surprise to* everyone.

348. When she was at her most successful, the princess enjoyed enormous popularity. (**HEIGHT**) → At *the height of her success*, the princess enjoyed enormous popularity.

Note(s): Study these noteworthy collocation patterns for *popularity*: *great, huge, immense, massive* (**adjectives**); *to achieve, to gain, to win* (**verbs**).

349. Although we were worried, it wasn't necessary because they had already come up with a solution. (**NEEDN'T**) → We *needn't have worried* because they had already come up with a solution.

350. I warned her not to be remiss in her duties, but I had no success. (WAS) → I warned her not to be remiss in her duties, but *it was to/of no* avail.

Note(s): Here are some noteworthy (near-) synonyms of *remiss*: *inattentive, neglectful, negligent, slapdash*. Opposite(s): *attentive, conscientious, mindful, punctilious*, etc.

351. 'Were you satisfied with the service, sir?' the waiter asked. (**LIKING**) → The waiter asked, 'Was *the service to your liking*, sir?'

352. He had the audacity, without any evidence, to accuse me of involvement in the fraudulent scheme. (**FAR**) → He went *so far as to accuse me of being* involved in the fraudulent scheme.

Note(s): 1) If you *go so far as to do* something, you are willing to go to extremes. 2) Here are some noteworthy (near-) synonyms of *audacity*: *cheek, insolence, nerve, temerity*, etc. Opposite(s): *bashfulness, timidity*. Related word(s): *audacious* (**adjective**), *audaciously* (**adverb**).

353. It was highly probable that Glenn would become an acclaimed actress. (**MAKINGS**) → Glenn had *(all) the makings of (becoming)* an acclaimed actress.

354. Sandra is by far the best student in her class. (**ANYWHERE**) → There is no *student anywhere near(ly) as good as* Sandra in her class.

355. Mark is far superior to me in terms of grammar knowledge. (**MATCH**) → When it *comes (down) to grammar knowledge, I am no match* for Mark.

356. The committee decided to postpone the examination, which was welcomed by all the candidates. (**DECISION**) → The committee's *decision to postpone the examination was welcomed by* all the candidates.

357. If you study very hard, the content won't be so difficult. (**EASIER**) → The *harder you study, the easier* the content will be.

358. The stranded cat would never have been rescued if the rescuer hadn't come up with an ingenious plan. (**INGENUITY**) → But *for the ingenuity of the rescuer's* plan, the stranded cat would never have been rescued.

Note(s): It may be worth looking at the difference between *ingenious*, whose (near-) synonyms are, for example, *creative* or *innovative*, and *ingenuous*, whose synonyms include: *credulous, naive, gullible, unwary*, etc.

359. Besides making you fit, there are many other reasons why you should do physical exercise. (**MORE**) → There *is more to doing physical exercise than simply/just* getting fit.

360. The teacher got angry with his students and started shouting at them. (**TEMPER**) → The teacher *lost his temper* with the students and started shouting at them.

Note(s): If you lose your *temper* very often, you are a *temperamental* person, that is to say, *capricious, moody, unstable*. Opposite(s): *dependable, easygoing, laid-back*.

361. They still haven't found out what caused the disaster. (**CAUSE**) → They have yet *to find out what the cause of* the disaster was.

362. Three actresses were competing for the leading role in the musical. (**CONTENTION**) → There *were three actresses in contention for* the leading role in the musical.

363. The spokesman for the government said that the information was mere conjecture. (**DISMISSED**) → The information *was dismissed as nothing more* than conjecture by the government's spokesman.

Note(s): In this context, *to dismiss* means *to reject, to discard, to brush off* (you can also say *to dismiss something out of hand*, with the same meaning).

364. Danny wasn't at all disheartened by that unpleasant experience. (**PUT**) → That unpleasant experience didn't *put Danny off in the* least.

365. Paul has hinted that he doesn't wish to remain in the company any longer. (**HINT**) → Paul has dropped **a hint that he no longer** wishes to remain in the company.

366. He was immersed in his reading, in such a way that he didn't notice when his telephone rang. (**WRAPPED**) → He was so **wrapped up in his reading that he** didn't notice when his telephone rang.

Note(s): If you are *wrapped up* in something/someone, you are so involved that you cannot pay attention to anything else; (near-) synonyms: *engrossed* and *immersed* (in a book, for example).

367. The ballet school is always looking for new talents. (**LOOKOUT**) → The ballet school is always **on the lookout for** new talents.

368. How does Anne earn a living? (**DO**) → What **does Anne do for** a living?

369. I'd say, in less forceful words, the students are a bit lively. (**PUT**) → The students are a bit lively, **to put it** mildly.

Note(s): 1) If you put it *bluntly* (as opposed to *mildly* – that is, *gently*), you say what you think in straightforward terms, maybe even rudely. 2) If you say something in less forceful words, you are being *euphemistic*.

370. I don't know why Tina made such a controversial decision. (**PROMPTED**) → I don't know **what prompted Tina to make so controversial** a decision.

Note(s): Or, more commonly: "... to make *such* a controversial decision" (note the position of the **definite article**).

371. I tried to be like one of my idols when I was a young teacher. (**MODELLED**) → As **a young teacher, I modelled myself on one** of my idols.

372. The team planned everything as carefully as they could possibly have done. (**UTMOST**) → Everything **was planned with the utmost care** by the team.

Note(s): Here are other interesting **adjectives** that collocate with *care*: *extra, extreme, great, meticulous* and *painstaking*.

373. I promised them that such an embarrassing situation would never be repeated. **(WORD)** → I gave *them my word (that) there would be no* repetition of such an embarrassing situation.

374. Coming second didn't make him feel any better because what Paul really wanted was win. **(CONSOLATION)** → Coming second *was (of) no consolation to him because/since/as winning* was all that Paul cared about.

Note(s): Study the difference between *to care about* and *to care for*. You care *about* the things you are interested in; when you care *for* someone, you love them, you provide for their needs, or look after them.

375. Jack finds that sometimes watching movies helps him stop thinking about his schoolwork. **(MIND)** → Jack finds that sometimes watching movies helps him *(to) keep/(to) take his mind off* his schoolwork.

Note(s): *Keeping your mind off* work/school..., etc. is important, so that you won't end up like Jack, from the old saying: "All work and no play makes Jack a dull boy".

376. I made an effort not to get involved in that awkward situation. **(MIXED)** → I tried hard to keep *myself from getting mixed up in* that awkward situation.

377. He announced that he would resign, and then said he had not been involved in the crime. **(WENT)** → After announcing his *resignation, he went on to deny having* been involved in the crime.

378. She realized that she was in a delicate situation and wasn't to blame for it. **(FAULT)** → Through *no fault of her own, she found* herself in a delicate situation.

379. I'm doubtful that this objective is really attainable. **(RESERVATIONS)** → I have *(some) reservations about/as to/regarding how attainable* this objective really is.

132

380. Francesca chose marketing rather than computing for her summer course. (**PREFERENCE**) → Francesca opted *for marketing in preference to computing* for her summer course.

381. I'd say you should practise eight hours a day. (**THUMB**) → As *a rule of thumb*, you should practise eight hours a day.

382. The demonstrators demanded that the government should ban animal experiments in the cosmetics industry. (**EXPERIMENTING**) → The demonstrators called *for a ban on experimenting with* animals in the cosmetics industry.

Note(s): 1) In the answer, *with* can be replaced with *on*: "... for a ban *on* experimenting *on* animals...". 2) The lead-in can be rephrased with the subjunctive (usually less common and formal in *BrE*): "The demonstrators demanded that the government *ban* animal..." (not "banned/bans").

383. 'I don't like how touristy Venice has become,' she said. (**LIKING**) → 'Venice has become *very/too touristy for my liking*,' she said.

384. Needles to say, I'm forever indebted to you for your support. (**SAYING**) → It goes *without saying that* I'm forever indebted to you for your support.

Note(s): *That* is optional here ("It goes without saying I'm forever indebted..."), but at CPE level you must use at least three words.

385. This event wouldn't have been possible without your unwavering support. (**MADE**) → Your unwavering support was *what made it possible for this event* to take place.

Note(s): 1) *Unwavering* (near-) synonyms include: *enduring, resolute, staunch, steadfast, unflagging, unswerving*, etc. Related word(s): *unswervingly* (adverb). Opposite(s): *irresolute, unreliable, weak*. 2) Some interesting collocations for *support* include: *complete, solid, wholehearted*, etc. (adjectives); *demonstrate, get, offer, receive* (verbs).

386. It's a pity the trainer made us believe that we were doing well. (LED) → If only *the trainer had not led us to believe/into believing* that we were doing well.

387. Disrespect is something that is not possible for me to tolerate. (PUT) → I find *it impossible to put up with* disrespect.

388. Even though the exercise may be hard, it helps to get your body into shape. (AS) → Hard *as/though the exercise may be*, it helps to get your body into shape.

389. I suddenly realised that I was making an unwise decision. (DAWNED) → Suddenly *it dawned on me* that I was making an unwise decision.

Note(s): You can also refer to an *unwise decision* as a *bad*, *poor* or *wrong* decision (collocation patterns).

390. At first I didn't want to go, but in the end I changed my mind. (HEART) → At first I didn't want to go, but in the end I *had a change of heart* and decided to go.

391. His menial job has never been an ordeal for him. (REGARDED) → His menial job *has never been regarded as* an ordeal by him.

Note(s): Some interesting (near-) synonyms of *menial* include: *demeaning, humdrum, lowly, low-status*, etc. Opposite(s): *noble, superior*, etc. As for *ordeal*, (near-) synonyms include: *agony, nightmare, torment, torture*, etc. Opposite(s): *contentment, pleasure*, etc.

392. University professors tend to feel superior to secondary school teachers. (LOOK) → University professors have a *tendency to look down* on secondary school teachers.

393. Let's go home. I don't feel comfortable at all at this party. (PLACE) → Let's go home. I feel *(completely) out of place* at his party.

Note(s): This is close in meaning to the idiom "a fish out of water": "Let's go home. I feel like *a fish out of water* at this party".

394. The girls were shocked to find out that Brad had stolen their money. (MADE) → The girls were shocked to find out that Brad *had made/run off with* their money.

395. We should always be grateful for what we're given for free, shouldn't we? (HORSE) → We should *never look a gift horse in* the mouth, should we?

396. In regards to fashion, he is a very discerning customer. (DOWN) → When it *comes down to* fashion, he is a very discerning customer.

Note(s): 1) You can often leave out *down*: "When it comes to fashion...", but make sure you use at least three words at CPE. 2) You can also refer to a *discerning* reader as *judicious, knowledgeable, perceptive*, etc. (near-synonyms). Opposite(s): *undiscerning*. Related word(s): *discernment* (**noun**) and *discerningly* (**adverb**).

397. You shouldn't worry about other people's safety while sacrificing your own. (EXPENSE) → You shouldn't worry about other people's safety *at the expense of your* own.

398. 'No matter what happens, I won't step down,' the president said. (MAY) → The president said, '*Come what may*, I won't step down.'

Note(s): 1) A (near-) synonym of *to step down* (= *to resign*) is *to stand down*. Both **phrasal verbs** collocate with the **prepositions** *as* and *from*: "... I won't stand/step down *as* chairman..."; "I won't *stand/step* down *from* power/my post...". 2) The answer may also be rewritten as: "Whatever may happen, I won't step down" or "(Come) rain or shine, I won't step down".

399. He almost admitted that he had lied before the judge. (MUCH) → He *as much as* admitted that he had lied before the judge.

400. 'The students' behaviour was nothing less than obnoxious,' the teacher said. (SHORT) → The teacher said, 'The students' behaviour was *nothing short of* obnoxious.'

Note(s): Here are some interesting (near-) synonyms of *obnoxious*: *appalling, disgusting, hideous, loathsome, offensive*, etc. Opposite(s): *agreeable, congenial, delightful*, *likable*, etc. Related word(s): *obnoxiousness* (**noun**), *obnoxiously* (**adverb**).

401. Even though I hold him in high regard, I have to disagree with him on this complicated matter. (**MUCH**) → As *much as I regard him highly*, I have to disagree with him on this complicated matter.

Note(s): The first *as* is usually left out: "*(As)* much as I regard him...". It goes without saying (but I'm going to say it anyway) that it means closely the same as *even though* and *despite/in spite of the fact that*.

402. 'Only you can sign this document,' my secretary told me. (**OTHER**) → My secretary said that the document *could not be signed by anyone other than* me.

403. In your opinion, does he have all the necessary qualifications to be in charge of the academic department? (**TAKES**) → Do you think *he has what it takes to be* in charge of the academic department?

404. The student stupidly started shouting at her teacher. (**HEAD**) → The student went *(completely) off her head* and started shouting at her teacher.

405. At the movie conference, I had the tremendous opportunity to meet the Meryl Streep in the flesh. (**NONE**) → At the movie conference, I met *none other than* the Meryl Streep in the flesh.

Note(s): 1) Less commonly, *no other*: "I met *no other than*..."). 2) We do not normally use the **definite article** before a proper name, but it is possible when we want to emphasize it. Also note that *the* has a different pronunciation in this case.

406. I always try to be hopeful, even if things will sometimes go off track. (**SIDE**) → I always try to look *on the bright side (of life)* even if things will sometimes go off track.

407. The student's success will depend basically on her commitment to her duties. (**MORE**) → Basically, the more *committed to her duties, the more successful* the student will be.

408. The twins are completely different from each other. (**RESEMBLANCE**) → The twins bear *no resemblance whatsoever/whatever to* each other.

409. The cats don't feel uncomfortable at all when the mastiff is around. (**EASE**) → The cats feel *completely/entirely at ease with* the mastiff around.

410. The student has a better attitude to school now that his teacher has spoken to him. (**IMPROVED**) → The student's attitude to school has *improved since he was spoken to by/after being spoken to by* his teacher.

411. He may seem a little bashful at first sight, but looks can be deceptive. (**OFF**) → He may *come off as* a little bashful at first sight, but looks can be deceptive.

Note(s): 1) Here are some interesting (near-) synonyms of *bashful* (*shy*): *aloof, self-conscious, unassertive, withdrawn*, etc. Opposite(s): *brash, gregarious, outgoing*, etc. Related word(s): *bashfulness* (**noun**) and *bashfully* (**adverb**). 2) You can also say "looks can be deceiving".

412. If this tense situation escalates, we'll have to call the police. (**COMES**) → If worse *comes to worst*, we'll have to call the police.

Note(s): 1) Alternatively, we say 'worst... worst' (both superlative forms); in *AmE*, we use the **article**: "If *the* worst comes to *the* worst...". 2) Also note these useful (near-) synonyms of *escalate*: *heighten* (height + en), *intensify* (intense + ify), *worsen* (worse + en); opposite(s): *decrease, weaken* (weak + en).

413. 'Have you forgotten everything about the accident?' she asked me. (**RECOLLECTION**) → She asked me, 'Don't *you have any recollection of* the accident?'

Note(s): (Near-) synonyms of *recollection* include: *memory, remembrance, reminiscence*. Related word(s): *recall* (**verb**).

414. It was so inappropriate of you to yell at your mother like that. (**ORDER**) → You *were completely out of order* to yell at your mother like that.

415. It is definitely not possible for me to ask her for support. (**QUESTION**) → Asking *her for support is out of the question* for me.

416. He asked me, 'Do you think I should go ahead with the project?' (**ADVISABLE**) → He asked me if *I thought it (would be) advisable to go* ahead with the project.

Note(s): A (near-) synonym of *advisable* is *prudent*; opposite(s): *imprudent, inadvisable, unwise*. Related word(s): *advise* (**verb**), *advisability* (**noun**) and *advisably* (**adverb**).

417. The teacher was very competent, and approachable too. (**ONLY**) → Not *only was the teacher competent but (he was) also* approachable.

Note(s): Two interesting (near-) synonyms of *approachable* are *congenial* and *personable*. Opposite(s): *inaccessible, unfriendly*. Related word(s): *approachability* (**noun**).

418. Peter showed deep regret, as he should have. (**WELL**) → Peter was deeply *regretful, as well he* might.

Note(s): At the end of the sentence, *may* is also possible ("... as well he may"). Also note these (near-) synonyms of *regretful*: *remorseful, repentant, sorrowful*; an interesting opposite worth noting is *unrepentant*. Related word(s): *regrettably* and *regretfully* (**adverbs**).

419. Since the concert has been called off, it would be better if we stayed at home. (**MAY**) → We *may/might as well stay* at home, since the concert has been called off.

420. You were lucky not to have come. The party is awfully boring. (**WELL**) → It is just *as well (that) you have not* come. The party is awfully boring.

421. I told you it was a waste of time to try to make him study harder. (**POINTLESS**) → I told you it would *be pointless to try* to make him study harder.

Note(s): 1) *Pointless* is usually followed by the **infinitive** with *to* (the **gerund** is informal). 2) Useful collocation patterns with *to study* include: to study *carefully, hard* (not *'hardly'*), *thoroughly* (**adverbs**); to study *under* (that is, *with*) (**preposition**): "She studied *under* the distinguished professor at university".

422. 'I wish you would stop making fun of me,' she shouted. (**JOKES**) → She shouted, 'Stop *making/telling jokes at my* expense, will you?'

Note(s): As has already been pointed out, after an **imperative** (affirmative), the **question tag** is usually *will*, but we can also use *won't/would* to convey politeness: "Stop making jokes at my expense, *won't/would you?*"

423. You can trust him with confidential information. He always keeps his promises. (**WORD**) → He is as *good as his word*, so you can trust him with confidential information.

Note(s): Learn this similar expression: *a man/woman of his/her word*.

424. Surely you agree with me that the Nobel laureate composes with flair? (**WAY**) → Surely you agree with me that the Noel laureate *has a way with* words?

Note(s): 1) Interesting (near-) synonyms of *flair*: *knack, mastery, panache*. Opposite(s): *inaptitude*. 2) Also note that *laureate* acts as both a **verb** and **noun**, with different syllable stress.

425. I wasn't expecting at all that you would stand up to the boss at the meeting. (**ABACK**) → I *was (completely) taken aback by you/your standing* up to the boss at the meeting.

426. Robert usually writes excellent compositions, but this one is a bit disappointing. (**MAIN**) → Robert writes excellent compositions *in the main*, but this one is a bit disappointing.

427. They wouldn't have rescued you without the help of the police dogs. (**HAD**) → Never would *you have been rescued if it had not* been for the help of the police dogs.

428. Apart from being a F1 champion, he was also very congenial. (WELL) → As *well as being* a Formula 1 champion, he was also very congenial.

Note(s): 1) In the lead-in, where you read "*Apart* from..." (that is, *besides, in addition to*) (BrE), *apart* can be replaced with *aside* in AmE. 2) We can refer to someone or a place as *congenial*, whose (near-) synonyms include: *agreeable, cordial, sociable*. Opposite(s): *aloof, disagreeable, unsociable*. Related word(s): *congeniality* (**noun**) and *congenially* (**adverb**).

429. The students were told to either keep quiet or leave the classroom. (NO) → The students were *given no choice/alternative but to* keep quiet or leave the classroom.

430. Shortly after I opened the door, a car pulled up near my house. (WHEN) → Scarcely *had I opened the door when* a car pulled up near my house.

431. 'Don't you think you should start behaving like an adult?' my father said. (THOUGH) → My father said, 'It's high *time you stopped behaving as though you were* not an adult.'

Note(s): 1) A potential error here is: "... time you would stop...". We use the **simple past** after "It's (high/about) time" + **subject**; 2) *Though* can be replaced with *if*: "... behaving as *if* you were..."; 3) In the lead-in, *like* (informal) can be replaced with *as* ("... behaving *as* an adult?"), but in the answer *like* cannot be used instead of *as*.

432. Have you ever attempted to write a book? (GO) → Have you ever *had a go at* writing a book?

Note(s): A similar expression is *to try your hand at*: "Have you ever *tried your hand at* writing a book?"

433. Surely the local papers treated the problem far too seriously? (PROPORTION) → Don't you think the problem *was blown out of (all) proportion by* the local papers?

434. People believed that the scientist's discovery would unravel the mysteries of the universe. (**BARE**) → It was *believed that the scientist's discovery would lay bare* the mysteries of the universe.

Note(s): (Near-) synonyms or *unravel* include: *clear up, disentangle, solve, resolve, sort out, unweave, unveil,* etc. Opposite(s): *entangle.*

435. Would someone please tell me what's going on here? (**LET**) → Would someone please *let/fill me in* on what's happening here?

436. 'I'll stand by you, whatever happens!' she promised me. (**THICK**) → She promised me she would stick *by/with me through thick and* thin.

Note(s): *Through thick and thin* means through good or bad times, no matter what the circumstances may be.

437. My phone was low on battery, but the passenger sitting next to me lent me his charger. (**LUCK**) → My phone was low on battery but, as *luck would have* it, the passenger sitting next to me lent me his charger.

438. Who could possibly have imagined that I would inherit anything? (**THOUGHT**) → Who would *have thought (that) I would come* into an inheritance?

439. Were Iguaçu Falls what you expected? (**LIVE**) → Did *Iguaçu Falls live up to your* expectations?

Note(s): Here are some verbs which collocate with *expectation*: *fulfil, match, realise, satisfy,* etc.

440. We got to the train station just on time. (**NICK**) → We got to the train station just *in the nick of* time.

441. Would you like to eat anything? (**CARE**) → Would you *care for something to* eat?

442. A life of hardship will be of no benefit to us. (**DO**) → A life of hardship *will not do us any* good.

443. They say strict discipline at school is beneficial for character building. (**WONDERS**) → It is <u>believed (that) strict discipline at school does wonders</u> for character building.

444. Could you help me carry this heavy box? (**TURN**) → Could you <u>do me a good turn (by) helping</u> me carry this heavy box?

445. I'm tired of all the hard work around here. (**DONKEY**) → I'm fed <u>up with (all) the donkey work</u> around here.

446. Benefiting from what I know now, it's easy to say that quitting was wrong. (**HINDSIGHT**) → With the <u>benefit of hindsight</u>, it's easy to say that quitting was wrong.

447. Machado's novels are the most extraordinary I've ever read. (**ONE**) → I've yet <u>to read an extraordinary novel as one of</u> Machado's.

448. She has not been seen for two days. (**SIGHT**) → No one <u>has had/caught sight of her</u> for two days.

449. They felt the candidate didn't meet the standards required. (**HAVE**) → The candidate was <u>felt not to have met</u> the standards required.

450. They didn't tell her what she should do, so she did it her own way. (**BEEN**) → Not <u>having been told</u> what she should do, she did it her own way.

451. Never before have I taught students who are so well-behaved. (**SUCH**) → This is <u>the first time (ever) (that) I have taught such</u> well-behaved students.

452. The idea was originally to publish the book by October at the latest. (**DUE**) → The book <u>was originally due to be published</u> by October at the latest.

453. It appears that the clients have received false information. (**GIVEN**) → The clients <u>appear to have been given</u> false information.

454. I want it to be clear to my students that I'm a tough teacher, but I'm fair. (SEEN) → I want to *be seen by my students as a teacher* who's tough, but fair.

455. It looks as though he has made a mistake filling in his form. (FILLED) → He seems to *have filled in his form* incorrectly.

456. She called in sick, so someone else had to substitute for her. (FILL) → Since she had *called in sick, someone else had to fill* in for her.

457. I did not hesitate to lie because I was just trying to help a friend. (QUALMS) → I have *no qualms about having* lied because I was just trying to help a friend.

Note(s): Some interesting (near-) synonyms of *qualm* (= nagging doubt) include: *compunction, pang, regret, remorse*, etc. Opposite(s): *conviction, self-assurance*, etc.

458. 'Please refrain from interrupting me while I'm explaining the content,' the teacher said. (BUTTING) → The teacher said, 'I wish *you would stop butting in (on me)* while I'm explaining the content.'

Note(s): Apart from the meaning *to interrupt* (from the lead-in), *to butt in* (**phrasal verb**) also means *to interfere*: "Stop *butting in*, will you? It doesn't concern you."

459. The officer's report and the defendant's version didn't add up. (ODDS) → The defendant's version *was at odds with* the officer's report.

460. Her friends regarded her so highly that she had everyone's unflagging support. (HELD) → Such *was the regard in which she was held* by her friends that she had everyone's unflagging support.

Note(s): Notice these collocation patterns with the **noun** *support*: *total, overwhelming, unstinting, unswerving* and *unwavering* (**adjectives**); *enjoy, give, lend, have, receive*, etc. (**verbs**).

461. There were thousands of angry demonstrators on the streets. (**PACKED**) → The streets _were packed with_ angry demonstrators.

462. My passport was stolen when I was abroad. (**ROBBED**) → I _was robbed of_ my passport when I was abroad.

463. The president has been given an honorary doctorate by Sorbonne university. (**CONFERRED**) → An honorary degree by Sorbone university _has been conferred on_ the president.

464. They believe a fault in one of the engines was behind the accident. (**BROUGHT**) → A fault in one of the engines _is believed to have brought about_ the accident.

465. The local people referred to the nurse as 'The Angel of Death'. (**DUBBED**) → The _nurse is dubbed_ 'The Angel of Death' by the local people.

466. The candidate finally took the presidential oath. (**SWORN**) → The candidate _was finally sworn in as_ president.

467. It's just possible that the students may need extra time. (**RULED**) → The possibility of _the students needing extra time cannot be ruled_ out.

468. You're not supposed to leave the examination room unless the proctors direct you to do so. (**ARE**) → You are only _to leave the examination room if you are_ directed to do so by the proctors.

469. I can't find my glasses. I know! I suppose I accidentally left them at the office. (**THINK**) → I can't find my glasses. Come _to think of_ it, I accidentally left them at the office.

470. The examination was shorter, but in fact it was more difficult than usual. (**RATE**) → The examination was shorter, but _at any rate_ it was more difficult than usual.

Note(s): Some interesting (near-) synonyms of _at any rate_ include: _anyway, in any case, nevertheless._ Also notice the less usual expression _all the same_.

471. He made a commitment to give up drinking alcohol. (**ABSTAIN**) → He took *a vow to abstain from drinking* alcohol.

Note(s): 1) Apart from *to take*, the following **verbs** also collocate with the **noun** *vow*: *to break, to keep, to make, to renew, to exchange* ("He *made* a vow to abstain..."). 2) From the **verb** *to abstain* we form the **noun** *abstinence*, whose (near-) synonyms include: *fasting, frugality, self-restraint*, etc. Opposite(s): *indulgence, self-indulgence*.

472. If the employees involved make one more mistake, they will be dismissed. (**DISMISSAL**) → One more mistake will lead *to the dismissal of the employees* involved.

473. I reject the biased notion that some people are superior to others. (**SUBSCRIBE**) → I *do not subscribe to* the biased notion that some people are superior to others.

Note(s): 1) Some **adverbs** that collocate with *to subscribe* are: *firmly, fully, wholeheartedly*: "I *wholeheartedly* subscribe to the view that racism is utterly abhorrent". 2) Some (near-) synonyms of *biased* include: *jaundiced, partisan, preconceived, tendentious*, etc. Opposite(s): *impartial, unbiased*.

474. Hawking was something of a legend, so to speak, someone all aspiring scholars wanted to be. (**WERE**) → Hawking was something of a legend, *as it were*, someone all aspiring scholars wanted to be.

Note(s): We can use *so to speak* with a similar meaning: "... something of a legend, *so to speak*", that is to say, "... something of a legend, (let's) say".

475. As we drove round the corner, we couldn't see the old mansion any more. (**WENT**) → As we drove round the corner, the old mansion *went out of/disappeared from* sight.

476. We need at least five people. If more people want to participate, we'll be happy, though. (**MORE**) → We need at least five people, *but the more, the* merrier.

477. 'Please don't go far, so I can see you,' the counselor told the children. (**SIGHT**) → 'Children, don't go *out of sight, will/would* you?' the counselor warned them.

478. When travelling abroad, you can't take it for granted that everything will go smoothly. (**ALLOWANCE**) → When travelling abroad, you have *to make allowance(s) for some* mishaps.

Note(s): Some interesting (near-) synonyms of *mishap* include: *calamity, casualty, disaster, hazard, mischance, setback,* etc. Opposite(s): good luck, success.

479. The prisoner, who was on parole, completely disappeared. (**VANISHED**) → The prisoner, who was on parole, *vanished/disappeared into thin* air.

480. 'In a war, while we're fighting relentlessly, who can tell who's right or wrong?' he asked us. (**THICK**) → 'In a war, *in the thick of the* fight, who can tell who's right or wrong?' he asked us.

481. Sometimes you have to turn a blind eye to your father's cantankerousness; after all, he's at an advanced age. (**ALLOWANCE**) → Since he's at an advanced age, sometimes you have *to make allowance(s) for your father's* cantankerousness.

Note(s): 1) (Near-) synonyms of *cantankerousness* include: *grumpiness, rudeness, unfriendliness,* etc. Opposite(s): *cordiality.* 2) You *make allowance(s) for someone* when you tolerate (*allow*) behaviour that you wouldn't normally accept from them because you believe there is a fair reason (for example, extenuating circumstances) to do so.

482. I don't believe what he says completely. (**PINCH**) → I take *what he says with a pinch/grain of* salt.

Note(s): *Grain,* instead of *pinch,* in AmE.

483. It was uncertain that she would pass her driving test. (**TOUCH**) → It *was touch and go whether or* not she'd pass her driving test.

146

484. Don't you think this is a storm in a teacup? (**FUSS**) → Don't you think you're *__making a fuss over/out of__* something unimportant?

485. According to Tina, Ayrton was simply the best in his field. (**NONE**) → According to Tina, Ayrton was *__second to none__* in his field.

486. John looks exactly like his father. (**SPITTING**) → John *__is the spitting image of__* his father.

487. I think you were trying something very difficult, considering your inexperience. (**BITE**) → I think you were trying to *__bite more than you can__* chew, considering your inexperience.

488. His discouraging words dampened my enthusiasm, so I gave it all up. (**BLOW**) → His discouraging words *__dealt a blow to__* my enthusiasm, so I gave it all up.

489. Years on end of not eating healthily have begun to affect her. (**TOLL**) → Years on end of not eating healthily have begun *__to take their toll on__* her (health).

490. Shouldn't we think about those who are less fortunate than ourselves? (**SPARE**) → Shouldn't we *__spare a thought for__* those who are less fortunate than ourselves?

491. Either you learn not to act too proud, or you'll get yourself into trouble at school. (**HEAD**) → Either your learn to keep *__your head down__*, or you'll get (yourself) into trouble at school.

492. If you're serious about getting into university, you'd better organize your studies more effectively. (**ACT**) → You'd better get *__your act together__* if you're serious about getting into university.

493. I'm not collecting money for myself, but for charity. (**OWN**) → I'm collecting money *__for charity, not on my own__* behalf.

494. It would be wiser to walk into town instead of driving, as there's too much traffic now. (**OFF**) → You'd *be better off walking* into town, as there's too much traffic now.

495. I cannot understand why Sheila divorced her husband in the first place. (**BEYOND**) → Why Sheila divorced her husband *is (completely) beyond* me.

<u>Note(s)</u>: 1) *Completely* may be left out, but no fewer than three words are needed at CPE; 2) The answer can be rewritten as: "... is completely beyond *understanding to* me".

496. You wouldn't mind posting this for me, would you? (**NO**) → Could you possibly *post this for me, if it is no* bother?

497. We apologize for the inconvenience. Please accept this upgrade from the airline for free. (**AIRLINE'S**) → We apologize for the inconvenience. Please accept this upgrade *with the airline's* compliments.

<u>Note(s)</u>: 1) Notice that, in the sense above, *complimentary* means (nearly) the same as *courtesy, for free*. 2) In other contexts, it may mean, among other things, *appreciative, congratulatory, eulogistic, laudatory, praiseful*, etc., as in "The critics have been very/highly *complimentary* about her new book". Opposite(s) (sense 2): *disparaging, reproachful, unflattering*.

498. I sometimes travel abroad on holiday. (**THEN**) → Every *now and then* I travel abroad on holiday.

<u>Note(s)</u>: Or: "Every *so often* I travel...".

499. Her desk is a mess, so she deserves it if she never finds anything. (**SERVES**) → Her desk is a mess, so *it serves her right (that)* she never finds anything.

500. Alcohol addiction almost destroyed her professional career. (**BUT**) → Her career *was all but destroyed* by alcohol addiction.

REVISE FOR CAMBRIDGE UNIVERSITY CERTIFICATES OF ENGLISH

LANGUAGE BOOSTERS 1 to 10

LANGUAGE BOOSTER 1

Advanced Vocabulary for Michigan Proficiency (C2), IELTS and TOEFL*

Below, you will find some words which may seem familiar, but some of them may have a different meaning from what you expected.

Also notice that sometimes, some of these words, when they belong to different **parts of speech** (**noun, adjective, verb**, etc.), have a change in meaning. Synonyms (or near-synonyms) have been given to help you.

abandon (noun) recklessness

accuracy (noun) exactness

adamant (adjective) stubborn

adversely (adverb) unfavorably

affluence (noun) abundance

to aggregate (verb) to amount to

allegedly (adverb) presumably

allegiance (noun) loyalty

to amend (verb) to perfect

to apprehend (verb) to understand

to augment (verb) to increase

belligerent (adjective) aggressive

bereaved (adjective) grieving, mourning

biased (adjective) prejudiced

burden (noun) responsibility

chimerical (adjective) fanciful, imaginary

clique (noun) clan, coterie

cogent (adjective) convincing

compensation (noun) reparation (damages)
consciously (adverb) deliberately, intentionally
constraint (noun) inhibition
consummate (adjective) perfect, superb
contemptuous (adjective) disdainful
to convey (verb) to communicate
convict (noun) prisoner
convoluted (adjective) intricate
decrepit (adjective) dilapidated
to deify (verb) to worship
deleterious (adjective) harmful
to depict (verb) to describe, to portray
to deplete (verb) to exhaust, to use up
derogatory (adjective) pejorative
despondent (adjective) sad
deviant (adjective) abnormal
to diminish (verb) to belittle, to denigrate
discrete (adjective) detached, separate
disenfranchised (adjective) disempowered, vulnerable
to dispel (verb) to dismiss, to repel
egregious (adjective) flagrant
entrepreneurial (adjective) ambitious, enterprising
erratic (adjective) unstable, varying
erudite (adjective) knowledgeable, scholarly
evasive (adjective) elusive
to evolve (verb) to develop, to unfold
to exalt (verb) to praise
expeditious (adjective) alacritous, quick

exponential (adjective) expanding
famine (noun) starvation
feasible (adjective) attainable
to fluctuate (verb) to vary
fractious (adjective) quarrelsome
fraught (adjective) packed, replete
gratuitous (adjective) uncalled-for, unwarranted
gregarious (adjective) sociable
hackneyed (adjective) clichéd, stereotyped
haphazard (adjective) random
hedonistic (adjective) luxurious
impervious (adjective) impenetrable
to implicate (verb) to incriminate
to impoverish (verb) to pauperize
to inaugurate (verb) to create, to launch
indisputable (adjective) unquestionable
industrious (adjective) hardworking
inherent (adjective) innate, intrinsic
inheritance (noun) heirloom
intermediary (adjective) in-between
intrepid (adjective) courageous
intrusive (adjective) meddlesome
invasive (adjective) meddlesome, nosy
jocular (adjective) humorous
judicious (adjective) discerning
lackluster (adjective) dull
loquacious (adjective) talkative
mellifluous (adjective) melodic, sweet

to mobilize (verb) to summon

nefarious (adjective) immoral

to overlap (verb) to imbricate

overwhelming (adjective) intolerable, unbearable

panache (noun) swagger, verve

parochial (adjective) narrow-minded

parsimonious (adjective) economical, niggardly

pious (adjective) puritan, reverent

portrayal (noun) depiction

precipitation (noun) impetuosity

predicament (noun) dilemma, impasse

prejudiced (adjective) partial, partisan

prowess (noun) dexterity, mastery

psychic (noun) clairvoyant, medium

reassuring (adjective) comforting

to recede (verb) to decrease, to subside

to reconcile (verb) to accommodate, to coordinate

relic (noun) corpse, remains

to resign (verb) to abdicate, to renounce

to retrieve (verb) to reclaim

secular (adjective) worldly (as opposed to heavenly)

tangible (adjective) palpable, perceptible

to unleash (verb) to release

unreciprocated (adjective) unrequited, unreturned

vestige (noun) relic, remnant

vitriolic (adjective) invective, outrageous

(*) Some of these words may also appear at Cambridge examinations.

LANGUAGE BOOSTER 2

COMMON PHRASAL VERBS AT B2, C1 & C2

Here are some highly frequent phrasal verbs you might come across at Cambridge exams. A (near-) synonym has been given, as well as a (near-) antonym, where appropriate. Note that "sb" and "sth" mean, respectively, "somebody" and "something".

to answer sb back to speak rudely to *sb* in return

to bargain for to expect

to be in for sth to expect trouble or retaliation

to bear out to support (for example, evidence) (near-) antonym(s) to invalidate

to bring sb up to educate, to rear, to teach

to call off to cancel (near-) antonym(s) to keep

to carry out to complete (near-) antonym(s) to interrupt, to stop

to come up with to think of (an idea/a solution)

to cut down on to reduce (near-) antonym(s) to squander, to waste

to do away with 1. to abolish (near-) antonym(s) to sanction 2. to murder

to do up to renovate (for example, a house)

to dawn on to realise, to understand

to drop out of to leave for good (for example, school)

to dwindle away to waste (near-) antonym(s) to save (up)

to face up to to oppose, to resist (near-) antonym(s) to capitulate, to surrender

to fall back on to have recourse to something

to get (a)round to to deal with something (after some delay)

to get along/on to be friends/on good terms with somebody

to get off/away with to escape punishment (lightly)

to give away to betray, to reveal (near-) antonym(s) to conceal, to hide
to give up to capitulate, to surrender (near-) antonym(s) to confront, to oppose
to lash out at to criticize (near-) antonym(s) to laud, to praise
to let sb in on sth to share (for example, a secret)
to let up to abate, to improve (of weather) (near-) antonym(s) to continue
to live up to to fulfill (near-) antonym(s) to disappoint
to look down on to despise (near-) antonym(s) to look up to, to respect
to look forward to to anticipate, to await eagerly
to look into to investigate
to look up to to admire, to respect (near-) antonym(s) to look down on
to make up 1. to invent 2. to constitute, to form
to make up for to compensate
to mistake sb/sth for (sb/sth else) to confuse with
to mull over to think carefully/hard
to play up 1. to not work well (of a machine) 2. to behave badly (of children)
to pull through to recuperate (from, say, an illness or surgery) (near-) antonym(s) to die
to put sb up to offer accommodation temporarily
to put yourself out to go to a lot of trouble (to help someone)
to see sb off to say goodbye (say, at an airport/station)
to set out (to do sth) to decide, to resolve
to splash out on to spend money extravagantly (near-) antonym(s) to save (up)
to stand for 1. to mean 2. to tolerate, to put up with
to stand in for to deputize, to substitute
to stick/stand up for sb/sth to defend
to swot up on to cram/to study hard (for an exam)
to take up sth to get into a new habit (such as a hobby or activity)

to tell sb off to reprimand, to scold
to track sb down to find (the whereabouts of)
to wear off to gradually disappear (for example, the effects of a medicine)
to wear out to drain, to exhaust, to tire
to work out = 1. to exercise 2. to calculate 3. to understand

LANGUAGE BOOSTER 3

IDIOMS (BY THEMES)

Below you will find some **idioms** commonly found at upper-intermediate level (or above), divided by areas/themes (animals, parts of the body, colours, etc.).

ANIMALS

ass ▸ to make an *ass* of yourself: *to behave stupidly*
bats ▸ to have *bats* in the belfry: *to appear to be crazy*
bee ▸ as busy as a *bee*: *having a lot of things to do*
bull ▸ to take the *bull* by the horns: *to face difficulties or challenges*
butterfly ▸ to have *butterflies* in your stomach: *to be nervous*
cat ▸ to let the *cat* out of the bag: *to reveal a secret*
chicken ▸ to *chicken* out of (doing sth): *to not do something because you are afraid*
cows ▸ till the *cows* come home: *to wait forever*
donkey ▸ to do the *donkey* work: *to do the humdrum, menial job*
whale ▸ to have a *whale* of a time: *to have a lot of fun*

PARTS OF THE BODY

brain ▸ to have a *brain* like a sieve: *to be forgetful*
ear ▸ to lend an *ear*: *to listen to someone sympathetically*
ears ▸ to be all *ears*: *to listen to someone attentively*
face ▸ to put on a brave *face*: *to try to look courageous and face a situation*
feet ▸ to be back on your *feet*: *to be physically/emotionally healthy again*
feet ▸ to think on your *feet*: *to make difficult decisions on the spur of the moment*

foot ▷ to put your *foot* in your mouth: *to say something you shouldn't because it's embarrassing*

hair ▷ a bad *hair* day: *a day when everything seems to go wrong*

hand ▷ to get out of *hand*: *to get out of control*

thumb ▷ to be under your *thumb*: *to have people under your control or influence*

COLOURS

black ▷ *black* mood: *to be irritable, angry, depressed, etc.*

black ▷ to *black* out: *to lose consciousness*

blue ▷ once in a *blue* moon: *happening very rarely*

blue ▷ out of the *blue*: *unexpectedly, suddenly*

colour ▷ to show your true *colours*: *to reveal your real nature*

green ▷ *green* with envy: *to be very envious/jealous (the green-eyed monster)*

grey ▷ a *grey* existence: *to lead a monotonous, uneventful life*

pink ▷ to be tickled *pink*: *to feel very happy or pleased about something*

red ▷ *red* tape: *excessive bureaucracy that prevents work from being done*

silver *silver* lining ▷ ('every cloud have a silver lining'): *unpleasant situations may have a positive side*

FOOD AND DRINK

apple ▷ to be the *apple* of someone's eye: *to be someone who you have great affection for*

beans ▷ to spill the *beans*: *to reveal a secret*

beef ▷ to *beef* sth up: *to improve something by making it stronger*

butter ▷ to *butter* sb up: *to treat someone kindly because you want to get sth from them*

egg ▷ to *egg* sb on: *to motivate someone to do something (usually some wrongdoing)*

milk ▷ no use crying over spilt *milk*: *to be useless to complain about something that cannot be changed*

milk ▷ the *milk* of human kindness: *to be very kind to everyone*

salt ▷ to take sth with a grain/pinch of *salt*: *to not believe sb or sth completely*

water ▷ to (not) hold *water*: *to (not) stand to thorough, critical examination*

water ▷ to tread *water*: *to be in an unsatisfactory situation that does not improve*

PLANTS, FLOWERS AND TREES

bud ▷ to nip sth in the *bud*: *to stop something from happening as soon as possible, before it's too late*

bush ▷ to beat around the *bush*: *to not speak your mind clearly because of hesitation*

daisies ▷ to be pushing up the *daises*: *to be dead*

grass ▷ to (not) let the *grass* grow under your feet: *to not delay in getting things done*

green ▷ to have *green* fingers: *to be good at gardening*

hay ▷ to make *hay* while the sun shines: *to take advantage of sth while it is possible*

leaf ▷ to turn a new *leaf*: *to forget the past and start living a new life*

roots ▷ the grass *roots*: *the ordinary people who make up the main part of society*

tree ▷ to bark up the wrong *tree*: *to do the wrong thing based on incorrect ideas or false beliefs*

trees ▷ can't see the woods from the *trees*: *to fail to see the whole because you are concentrated on (or distracted by) small details*

LANGUAGE BOOSTER 4

BINOMIALS

Some words and expressions always occur together, in a fixed order, forming **collocation patterns** (some may allow for change, but this is uncommon). Here are some **binomials** linked by the **conjunctions** "and" and "or". Make sure you use them where appropriate.

again and again (repeatedly) ▷ I've told him, *again and again*, to stop calling me names, but he just won't listen.

alive and well/kicking (still existing) ▷ Many thought he wouldn't survive. But I saw him the other they and he's *alive and well*.

an arm and a leg (to cost...) (to be expensive) ▷ This suit cost me *an arm and a leg*.

black and blue (bruised) ▷ The accident left her body all *black and blue*.

black and white (easy to understand) ▷ This isn't a *black and white* issue for me.

born and bred (raised) ▷ He was proud of being *born and bred* in old Edinburgh.

bread and butter (main income) ▷ I'm a freelance writer, but teaching is my *bread and butter*.

bright and early (very early) ▷ We have to be *bright and early* tomorrow, or else we'll miss the train.

by and large (generally) ▷ *By and large*, the event was a huge success.

down and out (penurious) ▷ Facing public disgrace, the Hollywood star was feeling *down and out*.

first and foremost (most importantly) ▷ What students need, *first and foremost*, is their teachers' recognition.

for better or (for) worse ▹ Nowadays, this is the tendency, *for better or (for) worse.*

give and take (reciprocity) ▹ In every relationship, there must be some *give and take.*

here and there (scattered) ▹ There's going to be rain *here and there* across the region tonight.

high and dry (helpless) ▹ After losing all his money in gambling, he was left *high and dry.* (figurative)

high and low (everywhere) ▹ The rescuers looked/searched *high and low*, but were unable to find the missing climbers.

hustle and bustle (noisy activity) ▹ Tired of New York's *hustle and bustle*, the family moved out to the countryside.

ifs and buts (no…) ▹ 'I don't wanna hear no *ifs and buts.* Just do your job, won't you?' she yelled at me.

ins and outs (the details) ▹ 'I don't really know all the *ins and outs* yet,' the detective said about the crime.

intents and purposes (for/to all) (in effect) ▹ The election hasn't finished yet, but for/to all *intents and purposes*, he is the elect candidate.

leaps and bounds (improve by/in…) ▹ The student has improved by *leaps and bounds* ever since his teacher gave him a scold.

long and hard (to think…) (for a long time) ▹ After thinking *long and hard*, he was able to make a sensible decision.

lost-and-found ▹ Have you tried looking for your keys at the lost-and-found? (note: in *BrE*, "lost property")

loud and clear (very easily) ▹ 'Can your hear me?' 'Yes, I can. *Loud and clear.*'

null and void (invalid) ▹ The judge declared the contract *null and void.*

odds and ends (worthless, small things) ▹ I have to get rid of some *odds and ends* when I clean out my car.

on and off (intermittently) ▹ It's been raining *on and off* all day, relentlessly.

once and for all (definitively) ▷ 'Let's settle this dispute *once and for all*, shall we?' he asked us.

once or twice (a few times) ▷ I called him *once or twice*, but he just wouldn't answer the phone.

one way or another (no matter how) ▷ He will find out the truth, (in) *one way or another*.

out and about ▷ He's *out and about* now after full recovery from the surgery.

out-and-out (in every way) ▷ The party flopped. It was and *out-and-out* disaster.

part and parcel (to be a part of) ▷ Feeling anxious is *part and parcel* of working in this field.

prim and proper (puritanical) ▷ Gloria is too *prim and proper* to engage in such intimate conversations.

pros and cons (advantages and disadvantages) ▷ I won't be able to make a decision until I have weighed the *pros and cons*.

pure and simple (and nothing else) ▷ All he wants is to take revenge, *pure and simple*.

rain or shine (come...) (whatever happens) ▷ I'll be there punctually, (come) *rain or shine*!

rank and file (the ordinary people) ▷ The party's *rank and file* are deeply dissatisfied with their leaders' arbitrary decisions.

safe and sound ▷ All the campers arrived home *safe and sound*, despite the bad weather.

said and done (when all is...) (all things considered) ▷ When all is *said and done*, it is your mother who will stick with you through thick and thin.

short and sweet (pleasantly concise) ▷ He kept his relevant comments *short and sweet*, as usual.

sick and tired ▷ 'I'm *sick and tired* of your feeble excuses. You are dismissed!' my boss told me.

so-__and__-so (person not named) ▷ 1. The two friends are always gossiping about *so-and-so* cheating on *so-and-so*. 2. (unpleasant person) ▷ Peter can be a real *so-and-so* at times, can't he?

sooner __or__ later ▷ *Sooner or later*, you'll realize that dropping out of school was a big mistake.

spick __and__ span (very clean) ▷ He takes pride in always keeping his office *spick and span*.

take it __or__ leave it (accept or refuse) ▷ That's all I can pay for your computer. (It's) *take it or leave it*.

thick __and__ thin (through good or bad times) ▷ They vowed they would stick together through *thick and thin*.

time __and__ (time) again (very often) ▷ I've told you *time and (time) again* not to forget to pay your monthly bills.

trial __and__ error (by/through) ▷ Most of what I know now was learnt through a painful process of *trial and error*.

tried __and__ tested ▷ In aviation, *tried and tested* safety procedures are key to success.

two __and__ two together (put...) (understand) ▷ When he puts *two and two together*, he's bound to find out what happened.

ups __and__ downs (good and bad moments) ▷ Every celebrity should be able to learn how to deal with the *ups and downs* in their careers.

wear __and__ tear (damage) ▷ Despite some *wear and tear*, the sofa is in very good condition.

wine __and__ dine (to entertain) ▷ The airline companies *wined and dined* potential clients in an attempt to have their loyalty.

LANGUAGE BOOSTER 5

DEPEDENT PREPOSITIONS (NOUNS, ADJECTIVES & VERBS)

Some **nouns**, **adjectives** and **verbs** always take the same prepositions, that is to say, these are **dependent prepositions**. Sometimes more than one combination is possible; or there may sometimes be a difference in meaning, as in, say, "shout at" (shout aggressively at someone) and "shout to" (in order to call someone's attention).

Nouns & Adjectives

advance on (noun)
angry at/with (adjective)
attack on (noun)
attitude towards (noun)
bad at (adjective)
capable of (adjective)
change to/in (noun)
clever at (adjective)
concerned about/with (adjective)
death from (noun)
delay in (noun)
dependent on (adjective)
deprived of (adjective)
devoted to (adjective)
difficulty (in) (noun)

disappointed at/in/with (adjective)
disposed towards (adjective)
eligible for (adjective)
emphasis on (noun)
envious of (adjective)
essential for/to (adjective)
expert in/on (noun)
familiar with (adjective)
foreign to (adjective)
free from/of (adjective)
friendly towards (adjective)
good at/with (adjective)
guilty of (adjective)
happy about/with (adjective)
hope for/of (noun)

ill with (adjective)
important for/to (adjective)
impression on (noun)
improvement in/on (noun)
incapable of (adjective)
increase in (noun)
independent of (adjective)
indignant at (adjective)
influence on/over (noun)
intention of (noun)
keen on (adjective)
key to (noun)
lacking in (adjective)
likelihood of (noun)
married to (adjective)
missing from (adjective)
need for (noun)
news to (noun)
noted for (adjective)
obstacle to (noun)
opinion about/on (noun)
particular about (noun)
poor in/at (adjective)
preferable to (adjective)
relief from (noun)
reputation for (noun)
responsible for/to (adjective)

restricted to (adjective)
restrictions on/to (noun)
result of (noun)
revenge for/on (noun)
rise in (noun)
satisfied with (adjective)
self-sufficient in (adjective)
sensitive to (adjective)
shocked at/by (adjective)
solution to (noun)
strict about/with (adjective)
superior to (adjective)
sure about/of (adjective)
surprised at/by (adjective)
sympathetic towards (adjective)
sympathy for/with (noun)
threat of/to (noun)
typical of (adjective)
victory over (noun)
views on (noun)

LANGUAGE BOOSTER 6

VERBS WITH DEPENDENT PREPOSITIONS

accuse sb of
agree on/to/with
allow for
amount to
apologise to sb for sth
appeal for/to
apply for/to
approve of
attend to
bargain for/with
beat sb at
belong in/to
benefit from
blame sb for
blame sth on sb
boast about/of
care about/for
change into
charge sb for/with
cheat sb out of
compete against
compliment sb on

concentrate on
confess to
confide in
conform to
congratulate sb on
consent to
consist of
contribute to/towards
convince sb of
crash into
cure sb of
deal in/with
decide between/on
declar war on
depend on
deprive sb of
die from/of
differ from
disapprove of
discourage sb from
dream about/of
end in/with

enter into
equip sb with
excuse sb for/from
explain to
feed sb/sth on
fish for
focus on
fool sb into
forgive sb for
grow in/into
guard against
happen to
have pity on
have sympathy for
hear about/of
help oneself to
hint at
inform sb of/about
insist on
interfere in/with
invest in
laugh at
mistake sb/sth for
object to
operate on
plead guilty to
prevent sb from

profit from
provide for/with
remind about/of
replace with
resort to
result from/in
rob sb of
seethe with
shout at/to
show mercy to/towards
speak to/with
speak of
specialise in
struggle against/with
succeed in
suffer from
surrender to
suspect sb of
think about/of
throw at/to
trust sb with
turn sb/sth into
wait on
warn sb about/against
watch out for
worry about

LANGUAGE BOOSTER 7

DO *OR* MAKE?

You *do*...	You *make*...
a *course*	an *appointment*
a (good) *job*	an *arrangement*
an *exam*	the *bed*
business with sb	a *call*
the (news)paper's *crosswords*	*coffee/tea*
damage	a *comment*
errands (tasks)	a *complaint*
physical *exercise*	*contact*
(an) *experiment(s)*	a *decision*
harm	(a million) *dollars*
your *homework*	an *effort*
the *laundry*	an *excuse*
research	*food*
sb a *favour*	*friends*
the *cleaning*	*fun* (of someone)
the *cooking*	a *fuss*
the *dishes*	*headway*
the *housework*	an *impression*
the *ironing*	a *joke*
the *math*	a *living*

the **shopping**	*love* (or war)
the/some **work**	*a* **mess**
your **duty**	*a* **mistake**
your **hair**	**money**
the **make-up**	*a* **noise**
your **nails**	*an* **observation**
karate	*an* **offer**
a **promise**	**progress**
a **reservation**	*your* **will** (testament)
a **suggestion**	*a* **wish**

LANGUAGE BOOSTER 8

RARE WORDS

Here's a list of rare words (or unusual, if you will), followed by translation into Portuguese, pure and simple, short and sweet. Be sure to use rare words cautiously.

acumen perspicácia, visão
bastion baluarte, bastião
burgeon prosperar (also: burgeoning)
conundrum enigma
convivial sociável
denouement desenlance, desenredo
edify edificar (edifying: edificante)
egregious flagrante, ultrajante
flabbergasted estupefato
fractious indisciplinado, rebelde
galvanize estimular, promover
imperious dominador
impetus ímpeto (also: impetuosity)
infatuation paixão (also: infatuated)
insouciant despreocupado
lackadaisical apático, indiferente
lionize idolotrar
myriad uma miríade de (coisas)
noisome repulsivo
odious odioso (also: odium)
paucity escassez, penúria
penultimate penúltimo
persnickety detalhista, mimado
philistine filistino (mente "estreita")
punctilious meticuloso
rapscallion biltre, patife
sanguine entusiasmado, otimista
serendipity acaso
timorous medroso
ubiquitous onipresente (also: ubiquity)

LANGUAGE BOOSTER 9

SIMILAR EXPRESSIONS IN ENGLISH AND PORTUGUESE

▷ *a light at the end of the tunnel* uma luz no fim do túnel

▷ *actions speak louder than words* ações valem mais que palavras

▷ *family ties* laços de família

▷ *full of life* cheio de vida

▷ *in good hands* em boas mãos

▷ *in the red* ▷ (estar) no vermelho

▷ *looks are deceiving/deceptive* as aparências enganam

▷ *not all that glitters is gold* nem tudo o que reluz é ouro

▷ *on the tip of my tongue* na ponta da língua

▷ *the black sheep of the family* a ovelha negra da família

▷ *to acknowledge receipt of* acusar o recebimento de (correspondência)

▷ *to bear false witness* prestar falso testemunho

▷ *to bear fruit* dar/produzir frutos

▷ *to bite the dust* comer poeira

▷ *to break the ice* quebrar o gelo (also: ice-breaker)

▷ *to buy an idea* comprar/apoiar uma ideia

▷ *to carry something too far* ir longe demais

▷ *to cultivate friendship* cultivar a amizade

▷ *to embrace an idea* abraçar/apoiar uma ideia

▷ *to exercise authority* exercer autoridade

▷ *to give cause for complaint* dar motivo/brecha/abertura para queixas

▷ *to have a screw loose* ter um parafuso solto

▷ *to have a short fuse* ter pavio curto

▷ *to have your whole life in front/ahead of you* ter toda a vida pela frente

▷ *to not lift a finger* não levantar um dedo

▷ *to pay someone back in their own coin* pagar/retribuir na mesma moeda

▷ *to play devil's advocate* fazer (as vezes de) advogado do diabo

▷ *to play with fire* brincar com fogo

▷ *to put one's cards on the table* pôr as cartas na mesa

▷ *to read someone's mind/thoughts* ler/adivinhar o pensamento

▷ *to run the risk* correr o risco

▷ *to save one's own skin* salvar a própria pele

▷ *(to not) see eye to eye* (não) se dar/"combinar" (com alguém)

▷ *to shoot yourself in the foot* dar um tiro no próprio pé

▷ *to take liberties* tomar liberdades (tratar alguém sem o devido respeito)

▷ *to take the liberty of* tomar a liberdade (de fazer algo)

▷ *to take one's hat off to sb* tirar o chapéu para alguém (em admiração/respeito)

▷ *to think big* pensar grande

▷ *to throw cold water (on an idea)* jogar um balde de água fria

▷ *to withdraw your remarks* retirar suas palavras / o que foi dito

▷ *ups and downs* os altos e baixos

▷ *with open arms* de braços abertos

▷ *without a shadow of a doubt* sem a menor sombra de dúvida

LANGUAGE BOOSTER 10

FALSE (AND TRUE) FRIENDS

No one wants a false friend, do they? But, unfortunately, they're around us and we need to be really careful not to stumble across some of them. On the other hand, sometimes there are true friends we just ignore because we never really looked at them more closely, so it's time we rolled up our sleeves and learned to tell them apart, isn't?

False friends

abort cancelar ▸ *aborto* (de feto) abortion, miscarriage

adept hábil ▸ *adepto* follower

advert comercial (propaganda) ▸ *advertir* warn

agenda pauta (de reunião) ▸ *agenda* diary, appointment book, planner

alias codinome ▸ *aliás* by the way

alumnus ex-aluno ▸ *aluno* student, pupil

amass (a)juntar ▸ *amassar* crumple, knead

anthem hino ▸ *antena* aerial

apology desculpa ▸ *apologia* defence

application inscrição ▸ *aplicação* (bancária) investiment

appointment compromisso ▸ *apontamento* annotation

appreciate dar valor ▸ *apreciar* enjoy, relish

assault atacar fisicamente ▸ *assalto* mugging, robbery

assume supor, pressupor ▸ *assumir* admit, own up (to doing something)

attend frequentar ▸ *atender* assist (sales assistant)

audience plateia, público ▸ *audiência* viewership

authoritative confiável ▷ *autoritário* authoritarian, overbearing

balance equilíbrio (also: saldo bancário) ▷ *balança* scales

balcony sacada ▷ *balcão* counter, front-desk

beef carne bovina ▷ *bife* steak

brave corajoso ▷ *bravo*: angry, mad

cafeteria cantina ▷ *cafeteria*: coffee shop, cafe

candid franco, honesto ▷ *cândido* (ingênuo) naive

casualty baixa (mortes) ▷ *casualidade* chance

collar colarinho (white-collar workers) ▷ *colar* necklace

college faculdade ▷ *colégio* school

complimentary de cortesia, gratuito ▷ *complementar* supplementary

comprehensive abrangente, completo ▷ *compreensivo* understanding

compromise entrar em acordo ▷ *compromisso* appointment (e.g. a dental appointment)

confident confiante ▷ *confidente* confidant

content satisfeito ▷ *contente* happy

contest competição ▷ *constestar* to object

conversant versado (instruído em algum assunto) ▷ *conversador* talkative

convict prisioneiro ▷ *convicto* convinced

costume fantasia, traje típico (costume jewellery = bijuteria) ▷ *costume* custom, habit

curse maldição ▷ *curso* course

dairy derivados do leite ▷ *diário* daily

data dados, números ▷ *data*: date

deception trapaça ▷ *decepção* disappointment

dependable confiável ▷ *dependente* dependant

discrete separado ▷ *discreto* discreet, reserved

discussion debate ▷ *discussão* (agressiva) argument (or: angry/fiery discussion)

diversion desvio ▸ *diversão* amusement, fun (an amusement park)
educated escolarizado ▸ *educado* (polido) polite
enchanted enfeitiçado ▸ *encantado* marvelled, mesmerized
enroll matricular, registrar ▸ *enrolar* roll up
eventually finalmente ▸ *eventualmente* occasionally (às vezes)
excited alvoroçado ▸ *excitado* (sexualmente) (sexually) aroused
exit saída ▸ *êxito* (sucesso) success
expert perito ▸ *esperto* clever, smart
exquisite excelente ▸ *esquisito* strange, weird
facility (-ties) acomodações, instalações ▸ *facilidade* easiness
gratuitous desnecessário, excessivo ▸ *gratuito* free
gratuity gratificação, gorjeta ▸ **gratuidade** free
hazard perigo, risco ▸ *azar* bad luck, jinx
idiom expressão idiomática ▸ *idioma*: language
indigenous autóctone ▸ *indígena* indian (from India, the country, Hindu)
industrious trabalhador ▸ *industrial* industrialized
inhabitable habitável ▸ **inabitável** uninhabitable
inscription gravação em relevo ▸ *inscrição* application, registration
journal periódico (revista) ▸ *jornal* (news)paper (impresso)
lecture palestra ▸ *leitura* reading
legend lenda ▸ *legenda* (de filme) caption, subtitle
malice maldade, premeditação ▸ *malícia* (licenciosidade) lechery, lewdness
notice anotação, observação escrita ▸ *notícia* (reportagem) news
notorious mal-afamado ▸ *notório* famous, popular (por algo positivo)
novel romance, novela (gênero literário) ▸ *novela* (televisiva) soap opera
particular exigente ▸ *particular* private (private property)
patron cliente, clientela ▸ *patrão* boss, employer

physician médico ▷ *físico* (especializado em Física) physicist
policy políticas (diretivas) ▷ *polícia* (corporação) police (force)
prejudice preconceito ▷ *prejuízo* loss
preservative conservante ▷ *preservativo* ("camisinha") condom, rubber
pretend fingir ▷ *pretender* intend
prohibitive (of prices) ▷ exorbitante *proibido* ▷ forbidden
propaganda propaganda (geralmente política) ▷ *propaganda* (televisiva) ad, advertisement
reclaim reaver, recuperar ▷ *reclamar* complain
record gravar ▷ *recordar* rembember, recollect
resume reiniciar, retomar ▷ *resumir* summarise
retire aposentar ▷ *retirar*: withdraw
retribution retaliação, vingança ▷ *retribuição* (recompensa) reward
reunion reencontro ▷ *reunião* meeting
senior idoso, superior (hierárquico) ▷ *senhor* (forma de tratamento) sir
sensible sensato ▷ *sensível* sensitive
silicon silício (Silicon Valley, California) ▷ *silicone* silicone (e.g. silicone implant)
support apoiar ▷ *suportar* tolerate, put up with
terrific excelente, fantástico ▷ *terrível* (horrível) terrible
trainer preparador físico ▷ *treinador* coach
travesty farsa, paródia ▷ *travesti* transvestite, cross-dresser
ultimately em última análise ▷ *ultimamente*: lately, recently
unique exclusivo, incomparável ▷ *único* (uma unidade) one
user-friendly: fácil de usar ▷ *amigável* amicable, convivial, friendly
valorous corajoso ▷ *valoroso* expensive

True friends

Don't be afraid of them. They *are* what they look like, even though some of them have been replaced with a (near-) synonym in current use/usage. By the way, we've given a (near-) synonym and translation. We have also shown related word(s), where appropriate.

assiduous indefatigable ▸ assíduo

calamity tragedy ▸ calamidade (also note: calamitous)

capitulate give in, surrender ▸ capitular, render-se

chronic incurable, persistent ▸ crônico

commence begin, start ▸ começar

contentious confrontational, fractious ▸ contencioso (de "contenda")

deleterious harmful, prejudicial ▸ deletério

deliberate intentional ▸ deliberado

discord disharmony ▸ discórdia (oposto: concórdia)

disparity discrepancy ▸ disparidade

dissension disagreement ▸ dissensão (also note: dissenter, a nonconformist)

diverge dissent, vary ▸ divergir

domicile abode ▸ domicílio

evasive ambiguous, misleading ▸ evasivo

exasperation vexation ▸ exasperação, vexação

expeditious efficient ▸ expedito (que tem expediente)

façade face, front ▸ fachada

foment promote ▸ fomentar

frugal economical, thrifty ▸ frugal

functionary civil servant ▸ funcionário público

imbecile idiot ▸ imbecil (also note: imbecility)

immense enormous ▸ imenso (also: enormity)

impede hinder ▸ impedir (also: impediment)

improvise devise, invent ▸ improvisar

incisive acerbic, mordant ▸ incisivo ("acerbic criticism" = crítica ácida)

indigent the poor and destitute ▸ indigente

indiscriminate eclectic, promiscuous ▸ indiscriminado

inevitable unavoidable ▸ inevitável (also: inevitability, inevitably)

infringe violate ▸ infringir (also note: infraction)

insinuate imply ▸ insinuar (also: insinuation)

intimidate coerce, frighten ▸ intimidar

medicine Medicine ▸ Medicina (mas também "false friend": medicamento)

molest harass ▸ molestar (also note: harassment)

omniscient all-knowing ▸ onisciente

palliative calming, soothing ▸ paliativo

prerogative privilege ▸ prerrogativa

prestige fame, reputation ▸ prestígio

procrastinate dawdle, delay ▸ procrastinar

prodigy genius ▸ prodígio

propensity inclination ▸ propensão

ptotocol code, rule ▸ protocolo (note the expression: breaches of protocol)

recuperate recover ▸ recuperar-se (de uma doença, acidente, cirurgia, etc.)

redundant excessive ▸ redundante (be made redundant: ser despedido do emprego)

retaliate reciprocate ▸ retaliar

studious assiduous ▸ estudioso

subjugate defeat, overpower ▸ subjugar

subtle understated ▸ sutil (also note: subtlety)

succinct brief ▸ sucinto

suffocate asphyxiate, smother ▸ sufocar

surreptitious covert ▸ sub-reptício

temperamental moody ▸ temperamental

tendentious bigoted, partisan ▸ tendencioso

tribulation adversity, affliction ▸ tribulação

tyrannical imperious ▸ tirânico

vehement ardent, fervent ▸ veemente

vicarious indirect, sympathetic (vicário) (vicarious experience, feelings, pleasures, etc.)

WORD LIST

This word list is made up of the words/expressions that appear in the Answer Key (explanatory notes). Just browse through it, making sure you remember what they mean. If you can't remember them, you might want to look them up in a dictionary. The **part of speech** (**noun, adjective, verb...**, etc.) has been given in the context of the examples. Some words may belong to more than one category.

abhorrent (adjective)
abolishable (adjective)
advisability (noun)
agreeable (adjective)
aloof (adjective)
altercation (noun)
answerable (adjective)
appalling (adjective)
assume (verb)
bashful (adjective)
blistering (adjective)
bluntly (adverb)
bothersome (adjective)
brash (adjective)
brush off (verb)
butt in (verb)
capricious (adjective)
chargeable (adjective)
come across (verb)
come/crack down on (verb)

complimentary (adjective)
compunction (noun)
confrontational (adjective)
congenial (adjective)
cordial (adjective)
cordiality (noun)
credulous (adjective)
deceit (noun)
delicate (adjective)
demeaning (adjective)
deplorable (adjective)
discerning (adjective)
discourage (verb)
disentangle (verb)
dismiss (verb)
disparaging (adjective)
dissuade (verb)
do away with (verb)
easygoing (adjective)
encounter (verb)

enforce (verb)
engrossed (adjective)
escalate (verb)
euphemistic (adjective)
expedient (noun)
fasting (noun)
forbearance (noun)
frugality (noun)
gregarious (adjective)
guise (noun)
gullible (adjective)
hasty (adjective)
havoc (noun)
hideous (adjective)
humdrum (adjective)
inconsequential (adjective)
indulgence (noun)
jaundiced (adjective)
judicious (adjective)
knack (noun)
knowledgeable (adjective)
laid-back (adjective)
laudatory (adjective)
liable (adjective)
liability (noun)
loathsome (adjective)
longanimity (noun)

mayhem (noun)
menial (adjective)
mindful (adjective)
moody (adjective)
naïve (adjective)
narrow down (verb)
neglectful (adjective)
negligible (adjective)
nerve (adjective)
nonconformity (noun)
noxious (adjective)
objectionable (adjective)
obnoxious (adjective)
opinionated (adjective)
ordeal (noun)
outgoing (adjective)
painstaking (adjective)
panache (noun)
pang (noun)
partisan (adjective)
perfunctory (adjective)
personable (adjective)
play up (verb)
praiseful (adjective)
presume (verb)
pretext (noun)
pugnacious (adjective)

punctilious (adjective)
put off (verb)
quarrel (noun)
quarrelsome (adjective)
reminiscence (noun)
remiss (adjective)
repentant (adjective)
reproachful (adjective)
resign (verb)
resource (noun)
run into (verb)
scorching (adjective)
self-conscious (adjective)
self-indulgence (noun)
self-restraint (noun)
setback (noun)
show up (verb)
shrewd (adjective)
sizzling (adjective)
slapdash (adjective)
soar (verb)
sorrowful (adjective)
stand/step down (verb)
staunch (adjective)
stumble upon (verb)
surmise (verb)
sweltering (adjective)

tactfully (adverb)
take for granted (verb)
temerity (noun)
temperamental (adjective)
think up (verb)
thorny (adjective)
thorough (adjective)
crave (verb)
yearn (verb)
trustworthy (adjective)
turn up (verb)
unaccountable (adjective)
unassertive (adjective)
unbecoming (adjective)
unbiased (adjective)
uncompromising (adjective)
unflagging (adjective)
unflattering (adjective)
unseemly (adjective)
unswerving (adjective)
untoward (adjective)
unveil (verb)
unwary (adjective)
unwavering (adjective)
unweave (verb)
unwise (adjective)
unyielding (adjective)

wind up (verb)
withdrawn (adjective)
wrapped up (adjective)

BIBLIOGRAPHY

Coursebooks (and other kinds of books)

ACKLAN, Richard. **Advanced Gold.** Peason/Longman.

BRADBURY, Tom; YEATS, Eunice. **Cambrige English Advanced 2.** Cengage.

GUDE, Kathy; DUCKWORTH, Michael. **Proficiency Masterclass.** Oxford University Press.

HARRISON, Mark. **Advanced Practice Tests.** Oxford University Press.

HARRISON, Mark. **First Practice Tests.** Oxford University Press.

HARRISON, Mark. **Proficiency Practice Tests.** Oxford University Press.

KLEIN, Virginia. **English Expressions.** Scholastic.

MADUREIRA, Ricardo. **Refresher Vocabulary and Grammar Tests.** Disal.

MANSFIELD, Francesca; NUTTAL, Carol. **Proficiency Practice Tests.** Thompson.

MARTINEZ, Ron. **Como Dizer Tudo em Inglês (Avançado).** Campus.

NEWBROOK, Jacky; WILSON, Judith. **New Proficiency Gold.** Pearson/Longman.

NORRIS, Roy. **Ready for CAE (and FCE)** Macmillan.

RODALE, J. I. **The synonym finder.** Warner Books.

SWAN, Michael. **Practical English Usage.** Oxford University Press.

VINCE, Michael. **First (and Advanced) Language Practice.** Macmillan.

Other sources

Cambridge University Press. **Official Papers.** (Printed editions).

Websites

Cambridge Online Dictionary

Collins Cobuild

Learn English Today

Longman Online Dictionary

Merriam Webster

Oxford Learner's

Thesaurus/Dictionary